BAPTISTS TOGETHER

Papers published in memory of

W.M.S. WEST, JP, MA, DTheol, Hon LLD
1922-1999

prepared for publication
by
J.H.Y. Briggs
and
Faith Bowers

**BAPTIST HISTORICAL SOCIETY
2000**

ISBN 0 903166 30 5

© 2000 The Baptist Historical Society

The Revd Dr Morris West

Oil painting by Louis Ward.
Photograph by David Bodey.
Reproduced here by kind permission of Bristol Baptist College

BAPTISTS TOGETHER

CONTENTS

Introduction	John Briggs and Faith Bowers	1
The Revd Dr Morris West: Autobiographical Material	Morris West	2
Memories of Dr West	Robert Ellis, Harry Mowvley	14
The Larger Context: Morris West, Servant of World Ecumenism	Keith Clements	19
A Few Words about the Christian Ministry	Morris West	30
Baptists Together: The Secretariat of the Baptist Union and effective denominational action		
J.H. Shakespeare	Morris West	35
M.E. Aubrey	Morris West	48
E.A. Payne	Morris West	64
The Child and the Church	Morris West	89
Bibliography	Anthony R. Cross	126
Index		133

INTRODUCTION

In settling to prepare the fourth and twentieth-century volume of the History of English Baptists, Morris West discovered that his own very direct involvement in the story did not allow him the distance required by the critical historian. Accordingly, he negotiated with the Baptist Historical Society to provide a personal reflection, leaving others to provide a comprehensive and critical history at a later date.

None of us had anticipated that Morris West would fall prey to terminal cancer as swiftly as proved to be the case. At the time of his death, this project was only partly completed. The three major chapters here presented, dealing with the secretariats of Shakespeare, Aubrey and Payne and covering the period 1898-1967, were left by him much in the format here published. In addition, he put on tape the details which appear as 'Autobiographical Material'. He also left some forty-four pages of notes for the volume he had planned. The first section of these deals with 'Baptists Together'. Where there is an indication in the notes that he had intended further material to be added to that written up fully, material has been taken from his notes and written up with the text here published. No attempt, however, has been made to 'write up' what he had sketched out for the history associated with the three secretariats since 1967. Beyond the secretariat studies, Dr West had planned further sections on 'Baptists at Worship', 'Baptists, Church and Ministry', 'Baptists and Unity', 'Baptists in Debate', and 'Baptists and the Local Church', but the notes were not sufficient for the editors to attempt to develop a text from them.

This tribute to Dr West also includes his essay, 'The Child and the Church: A Baptist Perspective', reproduced by permission of the Editors and Mercer University Press [*Pilgrim Pathways: Essays in Baptist History in Honour of B.R. White*, edited by W.H. Brackney and P.S. Fiddes with J.H.Y. Briggs, available in UK from Gracewing Ltd., 2 Southern Avenue, Leominster, HR6 0QF £35]. Also included in this volume are one of Dr West's characteristic ordination addresses and tributes given at his memorial service, together with a specially commissioned tribute from the Revd Dr Keith Clements, General Secretary of the Conference of European Churches, and a bibliography of Dr West's published works prepared by the Revd Dr Anthony Cross. The Society is grateful to both Dr Clements and Dr Cross for their support. Dr West's material is published by kind permission of Mrs Freda West, and the Society is grateful to her and to the Revd Dr Roger Hayden for locating his scripts and tapes.

JHYB and FB

THE REVD DR MORRIS WEST
AUTOBIOGRAPHICAL MATERIAL
As recorded on audiotape

Just a word of explanation as to what this is. It is not, I am afraid to say, a further instalment of Baptists Together. It is something that I think I need to do for somebody's sake, and that is to set down what only can be called frankly autobiographical material. A number of hours I have spent looking up details of people about whom I am writing or have to write memoirs of, and so on. I thought if I put it down all on one tape it would be of some assistance to somebody - and if not, will have done me some good.

I was born on 11th July 1922 in a nursing home in a house called 10 Oakfield Grove, which is, as a matter of fact, not only in Bristol, but within a stone's throw of Tyndale. The house still stands, but is no longer a nursing home. I was the third child of the family. My elder brother Griff was fifteen years older than I was, and my sister Joy ten. My brother and I never lived in the same house in my own memory because he went to boarding school before I was born, was at boarding school when I was born, and when he finally left boarding school at eighteen years old and I was three, he went to study medicine at Bristol University.

My mother was a Methodist whom my father had met in Bristol at the turn of the century when he came to the Baptist College and she was studying to be a teacher. She came of a very distinguished Methodist family called Schumm. They were Hanoverians who came over with King George, settled in Bath, prospered and were much involved in getting Methodism off the ground and knew, of course, the first generation of Methodists. There is a chapter on the Schumm family in the history of Methodism in Bath.

My father came of working-class stock. His father was a boot and shoe repairer in Northampton. My father left school, as they did in those days, aged about thirteen. He had to make his own way in the world. He became a sort of reporter for the local newspaper. He had several friends who became quite well known. One was a Baptist named Sammy Hughes (S.W. Hughes), a very distinguished President of the Union - a man who was also much involved in the Free Church Council movement and had good and long ministries, a fine preacher with a great sense of humour. He ran away from college when he was only a few weeks into his course and, as far as I know, he never went back there. Be that as it may, he became a leader amongst us and was somebody known to me. He was on the committee that interviewed me for the Baptist Union Scholarship in 1949. Sammy Hughes was a character and, although he was never a scholar of any sort, he was a thoughtful sort of person. Another friend my father had was very different. His name was Herbert Chapman and he became manager in the 1930s of the famous Arsenal side. My father had made arrangements to take me to see him at the Arsenal stadium in the 1930s, but sadly a fortnight before we were to go and see him he had a fatal heart attack.

My father worked his way along in the world of journalism and applied to Bristol Baptist College in 1899. He applied not from College Street, Northampton, which is where the family originated, but from Mount Pleasant, which was, I suppose, a sort of church plant and has grown, of course, into a very distinguished Baptist Church in Northampton. He was accepted by the college and stayed there until 1905. He had one year out, working in Queen's Road, Coventry, under Dr Blomfield, a very distinguished former Principal of Rawdon College. My father settled in 1905 at Zion Baptist Church, Bradford-on-Avon, Wiltshire. He served there until 1907, and often he told me the stories of the problems for people like him trying to get a move in the days before Superintendents. But he did move in 1911 to Kingsgate, Holborn, which of course is the old Eagle Street Chapel, that was later incorporated into Baptist Church House. He only stayed there for two and a half years, and in 1913 he went to Lower Edmonton, a working-class suburb in North London, where he ministered from 1913 to 1918, when he moved to Old King Street, Bristol. He stayed there until 1925, and it was during his time there that I was born.

When I was three years old, somewhat remarkably he received a call to go back to Edmonton. They had had a minister in between with whom they got on well, yet more than once during the years he was away - the seven years 1918-25 - they tried to lure my father back and he finally returned in 1925 and remained there until he retired in 1943. The house in which we lived was right on the edge of Edmonton and it was only a few minutes' walk up into fields and large houses - a much more rural setting, but things are very different now. We lived at 199 Bury Street and when I was five, coming up six, I was sent to a new elementary school called Raglan School which had just opened in a nearby suburb of London called Bush Hill Park. To that school I went from 1928 when it opened until 1931. These were days when a class was fifty pupils, taught from the front by one teacher. We learnt to spell, to read, to write and to add up – to do sums. It is extraordinary to think now how much we learned even in those days.

In the early part of 1931 my mother had to move down to Bath to look after my brother, who had graduated as a doctor by now and was going to marry in June or July 1931. He was a junior partner to a man who asked if he would kindly begin his work by opening up a new surgery on the east side of Bath. This meant my brother living over the shop and my mother went to keep house for him. At first I was going to stay at Edmonton, but evidently and very quickly it did not work so I had six extraordinary months down in Bath, where I went to an Old Maids' School which was fascinating, reminiscent of Joyce Grenfell. How much I learnt I know not, but I did begin to learn French and one or two other things useful to me later on.

My mother and father decided, when she had to come back to Edmonton, that to be brought up in Edmonton was probably not the wisest thing for their youngest child, and I think they were right. Although the neighbours were very nice, perhaps - if I could put it this way - the habits they had and the concepts they had would not have been particularly good in my own education. So in September 1931, as a nine-year-old, I went to Taunton School and there I was to stay for nine years. I enjoyed that. If anybody is interested in my school experiences, they are published. They are in a volume called *A Century of Promise*, published by the Old Tauntonians in 1986 or 1988 (I forget which). You can read my school story, as it were, of my school days there.

M.E. Aubrey was the first Secretary of the Baptist Union I met. He came to our local church and preached in connection with the Baptist Forward Movement in the 1930s. My recollection of him on that occasion is of his enthusiasm and his fluency. At the end of the service he stood in the front of the chapel by the communion table and invited all who shared his concern for the movement to come and shake his hand. I joined the queue, a youth of some fourteen summers. When my turn came, I recall he beamed at me, clasped me by the hand and said, 'Young man, welcome to the crusade'. The 'young man' bit made my day!

My last year at school coincided with the year of Dunkirk. Because I took School Certificate early, I had three years in the Sixth Form. I went in the Sixth Form in 1937 and was really anticipating going to University, but war had come and the great fervour and fever was to join up, as many of my contemporaries did. In fact, of those who entered the Sixth Form in 1937 with me, one-third never lived to be twenty-five.

But I did not go to University, neither did I join up in the normal sense of the word, because one Sunday evening in June 1940, just when I was beginning to take my Higher School Certificate, my father happened to be in conversation with one of his deacons who worked in a small arms factory in Enfield. He was bemoaning the problems they had there, for, of course, most of the weaponry had been left at Dunkirk or thereabouts. The factory was on a seven-day week, night and day shifts, in order to make up the loss, but they were desperately short of the skilled staff needed all over the factory. My father said, 'Well, I have a son whom you know, who is in training for science. Would there be an opening temporarily, while he sorts himself out, for him to work with you?' The deacon said, 'I'll go away and enquire if they need someone there'. My father said, 'I will go down to Taunton and ask him'. And this is what happened. My father came to talk to me and I said certainly, as a temporary expedient, I would have a go at it if there were a vacancy. My father got back and the deacon was eagerly waiting to tell him that the laboratory in the small arms factory at Enfield desperately needed someone competent in chemistry who would do certain work, make certain tests on the steel, and keep his mouth shut. My father thought that that suited me to a 'T'.

So before I took my Higher School Certificate I went up to Enfield, was interviewed and accepted. I returned to Taunton, took my Higher School Certificates, finished them on a Wednesday towards the end of June, left Taunton on the Thursday, and started work in the small arms factory on the Monday, at what I thought would be a temporary expedient. As things turned out it was five long years before I emerged from the work in factories. I was transferred in 1943 to an establishment in Poole and was involved in seeing off, as it were, the invasion force in June 1944. I will not weary you with the events of the war, save to say I was in London with my parents and sister throughout the London blitz, a never-to-be-forgotten experience, fire watching and so on and all the rest, and you literally did see fires in those days. Just to add that I did have one very interesting, unusual experience which was in fact broadcast and recorded. I appear on the 1945 VE Day celebrations in the television programme of 1995. If anybody wants to see that, they can find a copy and look at it.

At the end of the war I was clearly destined for ministry, I thought. Already in June 1945 I had applied to Bristol Baptist College. I was convinced of my call, like so many of the prophets in the Old Testament and many another since. The call came to me out of the context of the war. That is why my attitudes in ministry have been what they are - they have been shaped by the need for compassion, individual concern for everybody, reconciliation and community building. I was accepted to the college by Dr Dakin and his committee - a formidable committee, in those days. I was proposed and accepted as a student by Dr Rushbrooke, and seconded by H.L. Taylor, Treasurer of the Baptist Missionary Society. I went to college in 1945 and stayed for four years because I had to take, in the first year, classical subjects in the School Certificate to get a credit in order to matriculate in Bristol. In Bristol we enjoyed community life free from the travails of war, looking forward to the future - excited, stimulated by the teaching we got, and they were good days.

In the summer of '46 I went to Tottrell Bank to the BMS Summer School and there I met a young lady called Freda Metcalf. We were together for four weeks at that camp and at the end we were, as far as we were concerned, unofficially engaged. Freda and I went back to Tottrell Bank to help out for the next two or three years and then, in the summer of 1948, up in the Lake District I preached at Alveston Baptist Church - and Alveston was vacant. They wrote an encouraging letter to me, enquiring about my availability. I went to see Dakin with it. Dakin simply said, 'Rubbish! You are not going to do that. You are going with one or two others on to Oxford to take the Oxford degree. Let me hear no more about you trying to settle before you have been to Oxford for two years'. That was Dakin's way of doing things, and more often than not he was right. Certainly he was in my case.

So it was that preparations were made for me to go to Oxford, together with Harry Mowvley, Ray Taylor and Philip Winter from Bristol in the October of 1949. But there was a problem. Regent's would not accept married students. However, Harry Mowvley got a dispensation because he was a Regent's student anyway, studying at Bristol. He had already been engaged for ten years and even Robert Child thought that was a bit much, so he was going to get married and live in and leave his wife in Yorkshire. Freda and I decided to get on with it; there was a sense in which we had to get married, so towards the end of 1948 we decided to marry in the Christmas vacation. That's what we did on 1st January 1949.

In March each year, Regent's always played football against Bristol in Bristol. That year Ernest Payne planned to come down with them and would see the students who were going to Oxford in the following autumn. He met us all together, the four of us, and said to Harry Mowvley, 'I gather you have got dispensation to get married - a great rarity indeed'. Harry said, 'Yes'. 'But you will be living in, won't you?' said Payne. 'Yes', said Harry. Ernest Payne looked round with a twinkle in his eye and said, 'I take it none of the others of you are thinking of getting married?' I said, 'No, because I am already married'. Rarely have I seen Ernest Payne look more startled. 'Already married?' 'Yes,' said I, 'Dr Dakin said I could, so I did'. 'Oh! But you'll live in as well, won't you?' 'Yes', said I. So Freda stayed in Yorkshire for the two years I was in Oxford, where I took my Oxford degree.

1949-51 in Regent's we studied for our degrees, which we all passed in 1951. While I was there (or just before I went there, actually, in July 1949) it became evident that I was going to run out of money after the first year at Oxford because we all then got, if we had served in the war, five-year grants, and I had already used four in Bristol and therefore there was only one left for Oxford. So Payne directed me to the Baptist Union Scholarship and to the Dr Williams's Scholarship, both of which I got.

When I sat for the Baptist Union Scholarship, I met Aubrey personally for the second time. I arrived at the Church House in Southampton Row to sit the written examination paper. O.D. Wiles, the Assistant Secretary, welcomed me although it was clear to me that no-one had told him I was coming. With difficulty the question paper was found. The next problem for Wiles was where to put me to answer it. It was August. Many, including Aubrey, were away and no-one could invigilate. Then Wiles had a brain-wave. I should sit in the General Secretary's office with the door to his adjoining office ajar. So I sat in the General Secretary's chair at his desk and began the paper. About half an hour later the main door of the office opened and in walked Aubrey. Our consternation was mutual. 'Who are you?' he asked, with remarkable constraint. I began to explain when in rushed a flustered O.D. Wiles and explained. Whereupon Aubrey looked at me and said 'Well, young man, there *are* a few worse places to sit than in my chair - perhaps it is a foretaste of what may happen to you in the future!' Fortunately for the denomination (and for me) Aubrey's 'prophecy' was not fulfilled! But I was awarded the Scholarship and am glad to recall now Aubrey's kindly attitude towards me. I confess it has coloured my assessment of the man and in all that I have written about him I have been glad to bring him out of the shadows of both his predecessor and his successor into the light of Baptist history where deservedly he belongs.

So I went to Oxford and towards the end of the first year there Payne said to me, 'What are you going to do with the extra year's money you've got, because you don't need your first year's Baptist Union money until next year (i.e. 1950-51). What are you going to do in '51/'52?' I said, 'By that time I should be settled.' 'Ah well', said Payne, 'why don't you think about going to Zurich for a year - the University of Zurich - and studying there? Your wife can go with you; we'll find some money somewhere.' So we agreed. Then Payne came back to us and said, 'I've been thinking again, and speaking with Dr Dakin. You really ought to go to Zurich for two years and take a Doctorate. We'll find the money - Regent's will find the money for you for your last year in Oxford.'

So we did what we were told, and after my graduation we moved to Zurich where we spent two wonderful years. I studied with Fritz Blanke about the influence of the Reformation in Zurich on the Edwardian Reformation in England, particularly John Hooper, Bishop of Gloucester. At the same time I worked with Blanke in his initial studies and searches about the Anabaptist movement, including going round with him to find the farms where they worked and worshipped - fascinating stuff! Then suddenly, out of the blue, in January 1953 I got a letter from Regent's inviting me to go and take up the post of Junior Tutor and Bursar of the college. Mansfield and Regent's jointly were appointing Horton Davies, distinguished church historian, to teach Church History, and I would be his assistant. When we thought about it, we wanted to settle in a church, but I agreed.

Before I went to Regent's as Tutor I had a commissioning service in Edmonton Baptist Church on 30th September 1953, which was a Wednesday. It was entitled 'The Ordination to the Ministry and Designation as Tutor in Regent's Park College, Oxford'. The participants were extraordinary. The call to worship was led by the then minister of the church, H.W. Chapman, and my father. The service was conducted by Robert Child, who made a statement on behalf of Regent's, to which I replied. Robert Child also gave an address of sorts in his statement. Dakin presented me with a Bible and 'ordained' me - though he never put his hands on your head; he shook you by the hand and said 'Welcome'. But he gave the ordination address and the ordination prayer. After the hymn there was an address by Payne. There cannot have been very many people who had sharing in their service on the same night Child, Payne and Dakin.

So we spent the years 1953-59 - fascinating years - in Oxford. In the years in which I was Bursar we refurbished the jeweller's shop that we owned at 54 St Giles into a tutor's house, into which we moved. We also shared in the plans for the development of the quadrangle. I went and saw the Bursar of University College, together with our agent on the building side of things, to see if they would sell us the garage next door to Regent's so that we could develop further. We negotiated that and as a result the garage was bought. So we played a significant part in the life of Regent's just for those six years.

But then we thought we had had enough, so off we went to look for a church. There was no problem in finding one. Dagnall Street, St Albans, called me to the ministry and I was inducted to the pastorate at Dagnall Street on Wednesday, 28th October 1959. The service at St Albans was a somewhat low-key affair (compared with the ordination service). The charge to the minister was delivered by Henton Davies, who was by then the Principal of Regent's, and the charge to the church was given by Douglas Hicks. We had twelve very happy years in St Albans, great years. I had one or two feelers to leave St Albans, none of which I took. Gordon Rupp wanted me to go to Manchester to lecture in the university. Northern College invited me to the Principalship, which I did not take up. I was asked to go and preach in Yorkminster, Toronto, which I did not do. We stayed till '71 and, if you want to read about the time there, there has just been published a history of the Dagnall Street Baptist Church by Derek Turner.

Then in 1971 I was called to the Principalship of Bristol. In those days people were called to Principalships, they did not apply. It was a remarkable time at St Albans, but I came to Bristol, was appointed a recognized lecturer in the university, and for all my years in Bristol from '71 to my retirement in '87, and then for two years beyond, I lectured regularly in the study of the Reformation, having a great variety of students passing through my hands. To have the opportunity of lecturing both in college and in the university was a very great privilege to me and I greatly enjoyed it.

In 1958 I had been co-opted to the Baptist Union Council and I went on serving on the Council from '58 to '99.[1] During the time in Bristol, of course, my commitments to the Baptist Union increased still further and, looking back now over the years of Baptist Union service, I realize that I have spent many hours, if not the equivalent of days, in serving the Union. In fact, I once began to work it out and I reckon, counting a working day as eight hours, I must have given two years of my life to the Baptist Union on various committees and that, I think, is a low estimate. I chaired the Commission on Associations in the 1960s; prior to that, I chaired the Young People's Department, from about 1961 for a few years, which is when I became a member of the General Purposes Committee. During my time we had David Jackson and Dorothy Taylor running a very, very tight, efficient and effective ship. When David Russell came, I was chairman of the Structure Group, which restructured the

---

[1] Dr West was Chairman of Council 1982-85.

work at Baptist House and, although there was a lot of criticism of it over the years, it is very interesting to know that the threefold structure that we suggested at the beginning of David Russell's time is still the basis for administration, ministry and mission. I chaired also the Advisory Committee on Church Relations for some time, and was deeply involved in the 1970s with all the ecumenical shenanigans that went on with the 'Ten Propositions' and 'Covenanting for Unity' and so on. By the way, I should say that I was a member of the Group that proposed what is often thought of as the infamous 'Ministry Tomorrow' Report. Current reaction to it is largely due to the fact that no-one has read it in its entirety, for the crucial introduction to it, written by the Chairman, was not reproduced in the document booklet that Roger Hayden edited. Very few people, therefore, have judged the report in the context of that particular introduction which is very important to read.

In 1979-80 I was President of the Baptist Union and in 1981-82 Moderator of the Free Church Federal Council. This, amongst other things, took us to the wedding of Diana and the Prince of Wales, and to Buckingham Palace for lunch, and to the great reception prior to the wedding. Through the Free Church Federal Council, I developed further the friendship I had with Robert Runcie, Archbishop of Canterbury. He had been with me in St Albans during my days there where I got to know him well. He was President of the St Albans Council of Churches when I was Chairman. This friendship was a very great pleasure, as was getting to know that extraordinary Christian, Basil Hume.

In addition to that work for the Baptist Union, from early on I was involved in ecumenical functioning. As early as 1951 I went to a Faith and Order Commission Meeting at Clarens, just three years after Amsterdam. And you will find an account of that in my book on Ernest Payne. 1952 found me as a Youth Delegate at Lund for the Third World Conference on Faith and Order. For ten years after 1952 I substituted quite often for Ernest Payne, both at the Executive Continuation Committee of Faith and Order and on the Commission. In 1962 he resigned from the Commission because of pressure and because he was now on the Central Committee. This was at the Commission Meeting at Aarhus in Denmark. I was elected to the Commission and remained a member for twenty years. This meant that I attended the Commission meetings which were held, after Aarhus, in Bristol, Louvain in Belgium, Accra in Ghana, Bangalore in India, and, of course, Lima, Peru. Naturally I shared over the years in the work of producing the text of *Baptism, Eucharist and Ministry*.

I resigned in 1982 from the Commission but in the years that followed they used me from time to time. Mary Tanner and I produced, for example, the

Baptism section of the response volume to *BEM*. There was also a book that came out about examples of various liturgies amongst the churches, and there is one of mine in there which is not acknowledged as mine but you might as well know for the record that it is mine. That is the one to do with infant blessing and dedication. There are two in there: one, I think, from *Praise God* and another which is mine.

Talking about ecumenical commitment, I was involved off and on in the work of the British Council of Churches much earlier on, and shared as early as the late 1950s in ecumenical documentation and writing about the idea of initiation as a process. This went on, off and on, right the way through until 1995 when, of course, what is now Churches Together in England went on into the 'Called to be One' process. I did a document for them on baptism and church membership. The document itself was published in full in an ecumenical journal called, I think, *One in Christ*, and was taken up (some of the ideas, anyway) in a final report of the 'Called to be One' process. So that was another aspect of my life which occupied a fair amount of time but gave me the richest of experiences. Perhaps I should add that in 1975 I went to the World Council of Churches Assembly in Nairobi, which was a very interesting and good experience.

So my years at Bristol, with all this other stuff, were very busy indeed. But that is not all, because in 1964, when I was in St Albans, I was invited to become a magistrate. After consultation with the church, I became a magistrate in that year. When I was appointed there was no time limit. By the time I came towards the 1990s it was agreed, and rightly so, that magistrates retire at seventy. So I retired when I was seventy, which was in 1992. This meant that I had twenty-eight years as a magistrate. I think, when I was first appointed in '64, that I was the first Baptist minister to be appointed on to the bench as a magistrate. One or two other Baptist ministers have been Mayors, who automatically in those days were magistrates for a year. I am not sure when Stanley Turl became a magistrate, whether it was just after me or before me, but we were certainly the earliest. Being part of the magistracy, of course, involved a lot of other things as well. For five years I served as Deputy Chairman of the Bristol Bench which, when I joined it in 1971 was about eighty magistrates. By the time I left there were more than three hundred. Being Deputy Chairman was quite a demanding job: one supported the Chairman in many ways at special meetings and so on, and found oneself on various committees, including the Avon and Somerset Police Committee.

When I was on the bench in St Albans, I was a member of the Hertfordshire County Probation Committee. In St Albans I sat on the Juvenile Bench as well as on the Domestic Bench. When I came to Bristol I was put immediately on the Domestic Bench, which is very demanding. One normally never sat on more than the Main Bench and one other. So I became involved very quickly with the probation work again and from the formation of Avon, which I think was in 1972, when the old Somerset probation service and the Bristol probation service combined as the Avon and Somerset Probation Service, I became a member of the Probation Committee and remained a member until my retirement from the bench in 1992. During that time I served on the Prison Sub-Committee which oversaw, cared for and supported the work of probation officers in prisons. For about the last nine or ten years of my service I was Chairman of that Prison Sub-Committee.

Perhaps I should mention also, while I am talking about community involvement, that one of the most effective ways I found in St Albans of becoming involved in the community was through the Rotary Club. I became a Rotarian fairly soon after my arrival in St Albans, for both my father and my brother were members of the Edmonton Rotary Club. I greatly enjoyed my service to Rotary and, indeed, became President of the Club in St Albans in the late 1960s. When I came to Bristol I found that the Bristol Rotary Clubs were very different - much bigger, far more impersonal, and did not seem particularly interested. In any case I had not got the time.

I stayed at Bristol until my retirement in 1987, going on teaching in the university until 1989. During those years we entered into an agreement with the University College Cardiff that we should supply a lecturer on Church History for one morning a week. Initially Norman Moon did it and then I took over. I cannot remember exactly when, but it was well before I retired. As the work very much involved teaching students at the Baptist College in Cardiff, as a *quid pro quo* Neville Clarke used to come and lecture once a week in Bristol. It was a very happy relationship.

When I retired in '87, for reasons best known to the new Principal, they ceased having Neville over. Now I had committed myself to helping Neville by teaching Church History once a week until he retired. That meant that after my retirement I continued to go to Cardiff once a week for several years. Not only that, but I got an urgent plea with the breakdown of Barrie White's health to go and help out at Regent's, so for a number of years I also went once a week to Regent's during term. All this, together with the ongoing Baptist Union work, kept me busy in retirement. I also became Chairman of the

Superintendents' Board, which I undertook for four years. I was a member of the Pensions Committee, and then, somewhat startlingly, found myself Chairman of the Baptist Ministers' Fellowship. I got landed with the Chairmanship of the Search Committee for the successor to Bernard Green. Now I had already been on the Committee to appoint Bernard Green and Douglas Sparkes, and once again there had been pressure on me to allow my own name to go forward but I flatly refused. I could only be a stop-gap for a few years - it would not be fair on anybody, not least Bristol. But we had the work of appointing David Coffey, and then, somewhat surprisingly again, when the reappointment came up, I found myself in the chair once again.

Gradually I retired from Didcot, though, of course, I was deeply involved in the work to do with the sale of Baptist Church House in London and the purchase at Didcot. The sale was fraught and the minutes of the Joint Headquarters Working Group, which I chaired, make interesting reading. It was an adventure story. If anybody wants to get it orally, they should talk with Douglas Sparkes who bore most of the brunt of the negotiations. But the end product was satisfactory. By dint of skilful tactics and considerable pressure, the Baptist Church House was eventually sold. Initially there was tremendous interest in it until somebody from London Underground, I think, dropped the hint that maybe - just maybe - there might be a requirement to expand Holborn underground station to accommodate one of those cross-city lines that people kept talking about. They were going to link London terminals together. That was enough to put anybody off and all the other bidders disappeared overnight. In the end London Transport were persuaded to buy the House. They did so. The sale made some £10 million profit, and another million was added by investing it at good interest rates for a year. The Pension Fund and Home Mission Fund benefited by capital and a whole lot of other things became possible. When the work of the selling came to an end and we moved to Didcot, I was appointed Chairman of the Baptist House Directors, an office that I fulfilled for a number of years, greatly assisted by John Spiller, who had been appointed manager of the Didcot premises.

So there it is, if anybody is interested. That's about it. But it is a life that I am grateful to God for. A life full of busy-ness, diversity and very great kindness by other people. I had never realized until very recently when I became ill how much other people appreciated me and that adds to my satisfaction. So there we are. That will save people going fiddling around in search of the details for a sort of biography of Morris West.

MEMORIES OF DR WEST

Some additional biographical material was contained in the tributes by the Revd Dr Robert Ellis and the Revd Dr Harry Mowvley at the Thanksgiving Service at Tyndale Baptist Church, Bristol, on 11 November 1999.
Dr Ellis drew on the autobiographical notes, with these extra passages:

Morris was always deeply conscious of his good fortune relative to those of his peers who lost their lives in the war. Many of us here [at Tyndale Baptist Church, Bristol] will remember his leading worship a year ago at Tyndale on Remembrance Sunday, worship he led with a special sensitivity and which was for him personally poignant .....

Morris was to become a scholar of some renown in the field of reformation studies, and there were those who were to try and lure him into the secular academy. But his passion for the reformation was linked to his passion for the church's gospel, and his scholarship was always to remain directly at the service of the church and its requirement for able and well-prepared ministers. Morris' students, and all who ever discussed matters of theology and learning with him (whether in Reformation or in New Testament which he also taught from time to time), will have benefited from his ability to make the difficult concept clearer with an insightful and straightforward sentence. In the pulpit too he wore his learning lightly, a great preacher on his day, bearing God's Word faithfully and winsomely.

During his leadership of the College many students came to be grateful to him not only for his academic rigour but also his sensitive pastoral leadership and friendship. He was totally committed to the Bristol tradition of preparation for ministry summed up in the words of Caleb Evans which he loved to quote: 'forming them able, evangelical, lively, zealous ministers of the gospel' ..... Following the illness of his successor at Bristol he returned for a period as interim principal.

To coincide with the tercentenary of the College, the relatively young University of Bristol awarded Morris an honorary doctorate - a recognition both of his own scholarship and of the contribution made by the College through 300 years and in the more recent establishing of a Department of Theology in which Morris was a key person.

Morris became, of course, a leading authority on Baptist history, and his booklet, *Baptist Principles*, surely shaped the understanding of generations of those in ministry and the churches .....

Writing in a Festschrift collected in his honour by the *Baptist Quarterly* in 1987, one-time principal of the South Wales Baptist College, Neville Clark, wrote of Morris thus: 'So far as the Union and therefore its churches are concerned, Morris West has marginally nudged history. It is a verdict that can be rendered on few men and women in any generation.'

Morris' friend, Lord Runcie, recalls an incident on his visit to Bristol. Pursued by the press over some outspoken comments when Archbishop, Lord Runcie was calling at the College to see Morris. Morris opened the great oak door at the main entrance of the old college building and allowed Runcie to slip in before slamming it hard in the path of the pursuing pack. Turning to his old friend, Morris said, 'It's all right. You're amongst friends here.' I tell this story because there would have been those who would have seen the moment of brief fame - perhaps a statement on the steps, full of noble sentiments, to the marauding reporters. But not Morris. For him, those he cared about were always more important than any public moment or quick soundbite.

So this record of the public and denominational man is only half a story - and perhaps the least important part. Morris was devoted to his wife and family (on January 1st of this year [1999] Morris and Freda, with their sons Nick, Julian and Christopher, celebrated their golden wedding). He was a respected and much loved church member at Tyndale for twenty-eight years. He tried to avoid the limelight there, but served most ably as a church representative on the board of Bristol Churches Housing Association, and performed masterfully as the chair of the 'House Committee' of the housing scheme, which Tyndale had initiated. This task saw him combine to great effect his considerable pastoral gifts, his business acumen, and his ability to get people to do things! He led a home group for ten years until this summer, and he also headed up the team which edited and published the church's magazine and community newsletter. His counsel in church meeting was always wise and helpful - whether in diffusing an occasional tense moment, or in bringing the meeting back to the nub of an issue when it had (he felt) wandered away. It might also be said, lest too 'precious' a view of the man is emerging, that he would also on such occasions employ his wonderful sense of humour and - though the chair rarely heard the remark - the back rows would sometimes dissolve into giggles after one of Morris' asides.

Near the end of his life Morris looked back on 'a life full of busy-ness, diversity and very great kindness by other people'. And there will be many who look back on his life grateful to God for his kindness and vision, wisdom and grace. Here in the church where he worshipped, where we had the privilege of counting him part of our 'family', we mourn our loss of this fellow Christian pilgrim. The Bunyan window reminds us, as it did him, of our ongoing Christian journey and its ultimate destination. We celebrate this man, our man, used so marvellously by God over a whole lifetime - and strain to hear the echo of the trumpets sounding for him 'on the other side'.

The address by the Revd Dr Harry Mowvley:

It is a great privilege to be allowed to speak of Morris West as a friend and colleague of fifty-three years standing. I first met Morris in May 1946 when I entered Bristol Baptist College as a student, but it was after we returned from the long vacation in October that we became firm friends. Four of us, Morris, Ray Taylor, Philip Winter and myself all began our degree course together. Philip always tended to go his own way, but the other three of us lived, worked and played together for the next five years - three in Bristol and two in Oxford. 'Two's company, three's a crowd', we are told, but this threesome remained intact to the very end.

There were certain things about Morris which became patently obvious from the start. He was academically gifted with a sharp and incisive mind. He also had great gifts of leadership and his use of both these gifts was motivated in a very special way. A number of his school friends had been killed in the war while he himself, as a metallurgist, had been in a reserved occupation. He now felt that every minute of the life which had been granted to him was to be used to the full. It was a special gift which should not be wasted. That feeling permeated his life and work to the very end. Consequently, he gave himself to work totally, both then and throughout his life. This could have made him very difficult to live with but he was saved by two other factors - first, by his love of sport: he was a sportsman of no mean standing with great hand and eye co-ordination (down to cricket in the corridor with a hairbrush and a squash ball); and second, by a wicked sense of humour.

His father before him had been a student of the College and he had learned something of the Bristol tradition from him. In 1946 he kept the tradition alive, forming a link between the pre-war and post-war generations. Many years later he wrote a booklet on the Bristol tradition, in which he expressed his belief that tradition was not static but was constantly developing, based on the past but meeting the needs of the present and the future.

During the first long vacation he and Ray went to a BMS summer school while my fiancée and I went to a BU one. When we met again he had a girl friend with the same name as mine who lived only five miles from mine! He thus became an adopted Yorkshireman - well, almost! It meant that he spent a good deal of the vacations in Bradford and, since our fiancées were at work, we were able to meet to watch the cricket at Headingly or Rugby League or Speedway at Odsal. So we saw much of each other during vacations as well as in termtime. Oxford was reluctant to allow students to marry, though I had permission because I was a little older. Morris decided to take advantage of a more liberal regime in Bristol and he and Freda were married in January 1949 so that he could go on to Regent's as a man already married! My Freda and I followed suit in the July. Then the four of us lived in Yorkshire. Our wives occasionally visited us together in Oxford.

The third member of the trio, Ray, married in 1951 in Pontypool and the question was how we were to get there. It so happened that I had a close cousin living in the next road to Freda and Morris and he had a car. Morris could drive and so asked whether I thought my cousin would lend us his car for the weekend. He did so. The four of us plus clothes for the wedding travelled from Bradford to Pontypool, taking in the Wye Valley, and home again the following day. You could say that we had a time of close fellowship! In 1951 our ways parted. Morris and Freda went to Zurich for further study, not without some reluctance, for he saw his place to be in pastoral ministry. There was similar reluctance when he was invited to Regent's as a tutor but encouraged by his mentor, Ernest Payne, he accepted. It was no surprise when finally he entered the pastorate in St Albans in 1959. During this time we were all three busy with our own churches and had little time for personal contact, but our friendship was no less real for that; it was deep enough to survive without it.

When Dr Champion retired in 1970, there was little doubt as to who would succeed him and I, for one, was delighted to have Morris close at hand again. Norman Moon and I have often said how fortunate we were to work for so long in a place where there were no quarrels, no arguments, no tensions even, and Keith Clements shares that view. We did not always see eye to eye but we could talk about it and Morris usually had his way - because his way was usually right! All those qualities which I mentioned earlier were now brought to the service of the College where he was teacher, pastor, administrator, odd job man and anything else that was required. He brought with him something of the Dakin dislike of pomposity and false piety. Generations of students will remember not only his lectures, but his prayers, his sermons, his availability, his advice. He saw potential in people and expected them to reach it and would help them to do so. He had an eye for all that was going on around him and knew more about the students, their affairs, their relationships than they ever guessed. At the same time, he found time for the University, the Association, and the denomination, ecumenical affairs and for his local church here at Tyndale. Few of us who were present will forget the Tercentenary celebrations, the TV presentation, the University lunch, and the award by the University of the honorary degree of LLD which he accepted with great pride on behalf of the College.

Since retirement, there has been a little more time for socializing. We have had the occasional meal together. The three of us have met for lunch from time to time along with Freda and Mona. We have put the denomination right, we have compared the present with the past, usually unfavourably; we have reminisced; all things which elderly people are allowed to do. We did so again less than three weeks before he died. Yet Morris never really retired. His love of the College, his concern for the denomination, his interest in its history never ceased. So has come to an end a friendship which was deep and lasting, which needed not much socializing, but which was based on mutual respect, on common aims and ideals, and on that bond which cements people together, Christian love. We shall miss him, but we are here to give thanks to God for such a full life and for such a firm friend.

THE LARGER CONTEXT
Morris West, Servant of World Ecumenism[1]

In early January 1982 Bristol lay covered in snow and ice. On the first Friday of the Baptist College term a thaw suddenly set in. But while the snow on the roof melted, the down spouts around the library and chapel remained blocked with ice, and water began to pour through the library ceiling. What could have been a colossally expensive accident was averted by students and staff who spent much of the night shifting books to safety, mopping up, and risking life and limb on the roof (even a mountaineer with his abseiling equipment was called out to help) trying to divert the flood.

While all this was happening the College Principal, blissfully unaware of the chaos awaiting him, was still several thousand miles away, flying home from Peru. The Plenary Commission on Faith and Order had just concluded its quadrennial meeting in Lima. It had been one of the most momentous meetings in Faith and Order's history, for it had finally agreed on the text *Baptism, Eucharist and Ministry* to be presented to the world's churches as an expression of the degree of 'convergence' on these central matters after more than thirty years of study and discussion. Morris West had in varying ways been party to the process throughout those years and felt that to have been present to experience this 'ecumenical miracle', as he called it, was a crowning privilege.

From the rarified heights of an international ecumenical encounter to a sodden and dishevelled library back in his own college community: Morris West, typically, took the transition in his stride and very soon life was back to normal. In fact 'normality' seemed to accompany him almost everywhere. Many a student (and sometimes staff as well) will recall hurrying to confront him in his study with some sudden emergency, only to find the 'crisis' de-dramatized as he leant backward in his chair, hawkish nose toward the ceiling, hands behind his head, and asked slowly, almost hesitantly, 'Now, tell me, what is the actual situation . . .' He was fond of pointing out that in *Hamlet* no character is more important on that stage filled with angst and villainy than the matter-of-fact, sensible Horatio who represents order and purpose - 'Heaven will direct it' - when the rest of the world seems to be falling apart.

---

[1] *NB: The author is grateful for recollections and comments from Dr Lukas Vischer, Revd J.F.V. Nicholson, Canon Martin Reardon and Dr Mary Tanner.*

There are those who remain locked in their particular contexts of locality and denomination, affecting to dismiss (perhaps out of envy, or fear) involvement on the wider scene. There are those who are only too happy to play in the international arena as a means of escape from the seemingly trivial round and common task at home. Morris West, however, was equally at home in both worlds. To him both were important. Neither was to be played off against the other, both needed the resourcing and challenge which one provided to the other, each had meaning only in the light of the other. In each the work of God was to be done and in that sense each was crucially important - and therefore 'normal'. It was in his steadfast pursuit of this bipolar integrity that he made his special contribution as a Baptist ecumenical and an ecumenical Baptist. Neville Clark in his elegant, wittily nuanced, 1987 essay on Morris West has already paid perceptive tribute to a 'Servant of the Union' and to the ecumenical dimension which he brought into that denominational service.[2] All this present essay aims to do is to provide some enlargement, and up-dating, on Morris West's main ecumenical contribution.

To gauge the full measure of his ecumenical life and thinking, we should start at the beginning. Though son of a Baptist manse, and ever a committed Baptist, it was his experience of life in the world rather than in the church which drew him towards Christian ministry. 'During the war I came into contact with all sorts and conditions of men and began to realize the need for the proclamation of the Christian gospel.'[3] He had left Taunton School in 1940 to work as a metallurgist. In vain did he try to escape into the Royal Air Force: he was accepted for training as a navigator in Bomber Command but his work (perhaps fortunately for his own survival) was declared a 'reserved occupation'. Both at Bristol and at Oxford his teachers (and fellow students) included others than Baptists - while chief among his Baptist mentors at Regent's Park was Ernest Payne,[4] already an established figure on the ecumenical stage and even then on the look-out for protégés to take up the mantle in due course. Moreover when he went to Zurich in 1951 to study church history under Fritz Blanke, and to encounter the great duo of Eduard Schweizer and Emil Brunner, the subject of his doctoral dissertation was that

---

[2] N. Clark, 'Servant of the Union', in J. Briggs (ed.), *Faith, Heritage and Witness*, Baptist Historical Society 1987, pp.13-20.

[3] 'Curriculum Vitae' appended to doctoral dissertation (see n.4).

[4] Cf Morris West's own biography of E.A. Payne, *To be a Pilgrim*, Lutterworth Press 1983.

seminal and tragic reforming figure in the Church of England, Bishop John Hooper.[5] The thrust of his thesis was that while most contemporary accounts of the English reformation still ascribed the origins of Puritanism to the influence of Calvin's Geneva, through Hooper the Zurich of Zwingli and Bullinger had also left an indelible mark in England. This was an invitation to take a larger, more inclusive view of historical influences on church life. Morris West may, therefore, from the beginning be described as an ecumenical scholar both in his interests and his particular approach: seeking the larger view. His time as Tutor at Regent's Park College (1953-59) also inevitably meant that as a university teacher he related to students and colleagues of diverse backgrounds. On many an afternoon he shared the paternal duty of propelling an infant push-chair round the Parks with a young Anglican don by the name of David Jenkins.

It was in fact while embarking on and continuing his study at Zurich that Morris West also had his first encounters with the more structured ecumenical activity of the Faith and Order movement. In 1951 at Clarens in Switzerland, as a youth delegate, he joined fellow-Baptists, Ernest Payne and C.T. LeQuesne, for the meeting of the Faith and Order Commission, and the following year, again as a youth delegate, he attended the 3rd World Conference on Faith and Order at Lund, Sweden.[6] Both through scholarship and experience, therefore, he was finding his feet on the international ecumenical scene at a relatively early age. Not that he immediately appeared in a starring or even a regular supporting role (he did not, for example, attend the 4th World Conference on Faith and Order in Montreal, 1963). For a decade he concentrated his efforts on where he felt he first belonged, as college tutor and then as local church pastor in St Albans. But the ecumenical commitment was always evident, as in his advocacy of the cause in the Baptist Union Council and as a Baptist representative on the British Council of Churches, and through his activities at local level in St Albans where a close friendship with Bishop - future Archbishop of Canterbury - Robert Runcie blossomed.

In 1964, Ernest Payne resigned from the Plenary Commission of Faith and Order due to the rising pressure of his other ecumenical commitments, and

---

[5] W.M.S. West, *John Hooper and the Origins of Puritanism*, doctoral dissertation, University of Zurich. Printed 1955 for private circulation.

[6] Much of the ensuing story, though he keeps himself well hidden from view, is to be read between the lines of Morris West's essay 'Baptists in Faith and Order - a Study in Baptismal Convergence', in K.W. Clements (ed.), *Baptists in the Twentieth Century*, Baptist Historical Society 1983.

at its meeting in Aarhus, Denmark, that year Morris West took his place. He had now found his ideal theological milieu. The contributions of other Baptists, such as L.G. Champion and G.R. Beasley-Murray from England, and Günther Wagner of Rüschlikon, to Faith and Order work were also highly important. Morris West, however, over the next twenty years moved towards the heart of the Commission's work in a special way. The Plenary Commission is a relatively large body with well over 100 members, meeting about every four years. Much of the real, continual influence in Faith and Order is exercised by the much smaller Standing Commission[7] which meets annually. It was at the meeting of the Plenary Commission at Louvain in 1971 that Morris West was elected to this inner caucus on which he remained until 1983. Louvain, however, was important in several other respects, not least in the decision that the time had come, drawing on the fruits of years of study and discussion, to develop a 'consensus' document on baptism, eucharist and ministry. Thus was set in train the process leading to the 1982 Lima text, *Baptism, Eucharist and Ministry*, the most widely publicized and discussed ecumenical document of the twentieth century. Morris West was to be at the heart of this process, and in much of its follow-up. His role therefore needs to be sketched here, while not forgetting other Faith and Order themes of the 1970s to which we will turn later.

In the years immediately following the 1963 Montreal conference, baptism had received relatively little attention in Faith and Order. It was at the 1967 Plenary Commission meeting in Bristol that the then Director of Faith and Order, Lukas Vischer, warned that the current focus on the eucharist must be widened to consider the relationship of that sacrament with baptism. When the Commission next met at Louvain it therefore had before it a report, *Baptism, Confirmation and Eucharist*, in the preparation of which Günther Wagner had made a major contribution. Morris West always regarded this report and the discussion of it at Louvain as providing the crucial impulse to the whole *BEM* story, and for two main reasons. First, there was the recognition that the *practice* of baptism - pastorally and liturgically - had to be examined no less than the 'theology'. Second, baptismal practices had to be viewed in relation to their particular *contexts*, social and cultural no less than confessional. This realization greatly arrested Morris West himself as he empathized with the special difficulties facing churches in, for instance, the officially atheist culture of the German Democratic Republic or the caste system in India.

After Louvain a number of documents on the attempt to reach a consensus

---

[7] Until 1975 it was in fact called the 'Working Committee'.

on baptism were circulated to the churches for comment, and work began also on the eucharist and ministry. Morris West was fully involved in the Standing Commission's annual supervision of this process. The next Plenary Commission meeting in Accra, Ghana, in 1974 drafted a first consensus document on baptism, eucharist and ministry. It was generated out of considerable and at times difficult discussion, with Baptists in particular uneasy at what they felt to be rather glib talk of our unity in a 'common baptism'. Indeed, it was becoming clear that 'consensus' was itself a rather misleading term, when at the most what could be hoped for was a summary of shared convictions and perspectives. Clearly the process had reached a critical stage. It was even decided to 'suspend' work on the three-fold study, but the report *Baptism, One Eucharist and a Mutually Recognized Ministry* was put out to the churches for their reactions and was brought to the 5th WCC Assembly in Nairobi, 1975, which Morris West attended as a Baptist Union delegate.

After Nairobi, the Standing Commission was reduced in size and Morris West was now the sole Baptist member. He, therefore, had a crucial responsibility in keeping the direction and reviving the momentum of the baptism discussion begun at Louvain. The first version of *Baptism, Eucharist and Ministry* (*BEM*) was sent out to the churches for comment, and the churches' first responses were considered at a consultation at Crêt-Bérard, Switzerland, in 1977 and the Standing Commission meeting in Loccum, German Federal Republic, in the same year. The Crêt-Bérard meeting produced a document 'Towards an Ecumenical Consensus', issued in 1978. Morris West played an especially important role at Loccum, as moderator of the group dealing with the responses thus far to *BEM*, the proposed revisions and the form in which the texts would be presented at the Plenary Commission in Bangalore in 1978. Very soon after, another highly important stage in the baptism discussion was provided by the consultation organized by Faith and Order with Baptists, at Louisville, Kentucky, in the spring of 1979 in which Morris West participated along with fellow British Baptists, G.R. Beasley-Murray and J.F.V. Nicholson. This gathering reflected upon the Crêt-Bérard document and, perhaps more than ever before in the whole process, the question was faced whether agreement really existed on the meaning of baptism. For Morris West himself, what needed to be uncovered was the reality that beneath the differing practices of believers' and infant baptism lie not just differences about baptism itself, but differing understandings of the church. Recognition of the need to examine ecclesiological presuppositions has been hovering around Faith and Order's work ever since. In the recollection of one participant at Louisville,[8] throughout this consultation Morris West resolutely played the role of one who wished to set the foremost item of discussion in the wider context: to let justice be done to real differences while seeing that *both* traditions were recognizing initiation as a *process*, always within a believing *community* in which children had a real place, and always within a particular historical and societal *context*.[9] This perspective was to be liberating for the ecumenical debate on baptism, and to confirm the shape which the section on baptism would take in the eventual Lima text.

So to the Plenary Commission meeting in Lima in January 1982, when a new version of *Baptism, Eucharist and Ministry* was presented and, after further discussion and (mostly) minor proposals for revision, was unanimously voted to have reached a mature enough stage for transmission to the churches. It was indeed a great moment. For such as Morris West, however, this was not the end of the story. For one thing, his considerable skills both in diplomatic argument and in plain yet nuanced English usage had long been recognized in Faith and Order, and he therefore served on the drafting group which after Lima produced the final text as published.[10] It was eventually to appear in over thirty languages with a total printing of towards a million copies. In the opinion of Mary Tanner, subsequently to become Moderator of Faith and Order and more closely concerned with the future of *BEM* than any other British theologian, the fact that *BEM* was so unusually readable for an ecumenical text, and remained so even after translation, owed much to Morris West's drafting skills in the English original. Moreover, he was deeply interested in how 'reception' of such a text by the churches, with their varying understandings of authority, tradition and decision-making, was to be perceived. At Lima itself, he 'warned the Commission not to view the reception of *BEM* as a problem but to see it as an opportunity. He understood reception as a process by which the churches received the document for consideration, for use, and for a continuing response in dialogue with the Commission. Reception is a long process, he added. *BEM* was already part of a process of reaching consensus.'[11]

---

[8] J.F.V. Nicholson.

[9] Morris West's own reflections on Louisville are to be found in his 'Towards a Consensus on Baptism? Louisville 1979' in *Baptist Quarterly* Vol.xxviii (January 1980), pp.232-239, which is followed by the report of the consultation itself.

[10] *Baptism, Eucharist and Ministry*, Faith and Order Paper No.111, WCC 1982.

[11] From notes made and supplied by M. Tanner.

His own commitment to this process was evident in his speaking and writing, both within and well beyond the English Baptist constituency, in promoting the discussion of *BEM*. It is precisely here that his own perception of the nature of ecumenical discussion is striking. No one had been more central to the production of *BEM* than Morris West, no one was more ardent in its commendation and presentation to the churches. Yet at the same time no one was more prepared to point out its deficiencies, or at any rate, hidden under certain ambiguities, the gaps which the 'convergence' had still to close. This is seen most clearly in his own comment from a Baptist viewpoint on *BEM*, written for the Catholic ecumenical review, *One in Christ*.[12] 'It was,' he wrote, 'a remarkable experience to think back over the 30 years and recognize that one had worked in and through an ecumenical miracle'. Yet, to a Baptist many questions still remained unanswered, especially in the section on baptism: 'One of the difficulties in approaching and commenting on this document is, at one and the same time, to accept what it is saying to us in ways of challenge to entrenched positions, and yet to respond to it also as one who is true and faithful to the tradition in which one works and the positions of which tradition one upholds'. He repeats his concern for the ecclesiogical issue, and the central question for Baptists: 'whether the Lima document intends to suggest that it is the very performance of baptism which achieves [membership of the fellowship of believing Christians] or whether it is an act which illustrates that which faith has already brought . . . to the believer.' Similarly, to say with Lima that 'Any practice which might be interpreted as "rebaptism" must be avoided' would in its absolute form be totally unacceptable to Baptists.

Morris West therefore demonstrated that most difficult but creative attachment, a *critical* loyalty to *BEM*, during the post-Lima decade when there might simply have become a polarization between the euphoria of those who thought it had ushered in the ecumenical *parousia*, and those inclined to dismiss it as of little account because of its shortcomings. The remarkable total of 186 official church responses to *BEM* faced the Faith and Order staff and officers with a formidable if welcome task in collation and assessment during 1982-89. Morris West, as a member of the drafting committee, played a full part in producing the eventual report on these responses (continuing after his retirement from Bristol College in 1987),

---

[12] W.M.S. West, 'Baptism, Eucharist and Ministry: A Baptist Comment', *One in Christ* Vol 20 (1984), pp.24-30.

especially in the writing of the chapter on responses to the Baptism section of *BEM*.

Much of this account has focused on Morris West's involvement in the *BEM* process since this eventuated as Faith and Order's most conspicuous achievement during his years of participation. It was, however, far from Faith and Order's only concern prior to 1982 and it had vigorous rivals for attention. For example, much energy was devoted from Louvain 1971, through Accra 1974 to Bangalore 1978, to the project 'Giving Account of Hope'. This was an attempt to find an ecumenical unity in the declaration of the Christian gospel in the diverse contexts of human hope and despair in the contemporary world, in ways both true to the apostolic faith (cf I Peter 3.15) and impacting on the diverse contexts. My own recollection is that Morris West was at least as excited by this project as by *BEM*. It appealed strongly to his basic evangelicalism and to his down-to-earth concern for the everyday world. It also brought about a welcome intersection between the global and the local levels, since fundamental to the study was the participation of groups in very specific contexts. During the winter of 1973-74, one such group met as part of the Lay Training Programme at the Bristol College. Mostly lay, and representative of Baptist, Anglican, Orthodox, Roman Catholic and United Reformed churches, the group struggled with what the 'hope' of the gospel meant for their city today. The result in written form was a 'Conversation about Hope' which was published by Faith and Order and formed part of the documentation for the Plenary Commission at Bangalore, 1978.[13] Morris West sat in on nearly all these meetings (which were chaired by the present writer) as a consultant, never seeking to dominate, rarely speaking except when invited to, but fully engaged - and in turn, he acknowledged, being richly informed by the experience. He also spoke on the theme to the South West Ecumenical Congress held in Bristol in the spring of 1976.

Morris West was similarly engaged with the issue of 'conciliar unity', discussion of which was greatly stimulated by the report from Section II of the WCC Assembly in Nairobi 1975, 'What Unity Requires'. Again, he was concerned for local contributions to be made to this study, and once more, during 1976-77, a largely lay group (similar to the 'Hope' group and with some of the same members) met at Bristol College and submitted a paper to

---

[13] K.W. Clements, 'A Conversation About Hope', *Study Encounter* Vol.XI, 2 (1975), pp.10-16. See also the Bangalore 1978 report *Sharing in One Hope*, Faith and Order Paper No.92, WCC Geneva.

Faith and Order. One of his chief concerns, as always, was that the question of the form of unity should not be divorced from that of the larger context of the witness of the church in the world, and within Faith and Order he pressed this case with vigour. At the Loccum 1977 Standing Commission the minutes record him, rarely for once, making the first intervention in response to the proposals for a document on 'Church Unity' for Bangalore 1978: 'Dr West considered it essential that in the whole operation of moving toward the unity of the Church we must relate to Section I at Nairobi - "Confessing Jesus Christ Today". The main difficulty in achieving progress had been at the denominational level, not in Faith and Order or at the local level.'[14] In some ways the concern for unity to be linked with common confession was answered by the later Faith and Order programme, 'Towards a Common Expression of the Apostolic Faith Today', based on a new explication of the Niceno-Constantinopolitan Creed. Morris West, well after his retirement from Faith and Order (and from Bristol College), took a keen interest in this project and indeed played a major role in drafting the section on 'One baptism for the forgiveness of sins'.[15] This kind of project he considered central to Faith and Order. No less than in his dealings with his students, he was always watchful of any tendency for Faith and Order to do too many things, however worthy, rather than concentrate on what was absolutely essential and then see the wider implications of such essential work. During the Standing Commission meeting in Taizé in 1979, he spoke forthrightly on the need to exercise rigorous discipline in resisting the temptations of an expanding agenda: 'We have a lot of hares running and should seek to fix the highest priorities. We should also make sure we have a programme geared to our main purpose of helping the churches to reach unity.'[16]

After retiring from the Faith and Order Commission in 1983 Morris West, as already made clear, remained committed and ready to help as consultant, adviser and writer. His last main piece of service in this area was at national level, when he served as consultant to the Churches Together in England working party which in 1997 produced the report *Baptism and Church Membership*.[17] At first diffident about being called on, yet again, to play the role of elder statesman, he nevertheless attended practically all the meetings

---

[14] Loccum Minutes, Faith and Order Paper No.83, WCC 1977, p.6.

[15] Confessing the One Faith. An Explication of the Apostolic Faith as it is Confessed in the Niceno-Constantinopolitan Creed (381), Faith and Order Paper No.153, WCC 1991.

[16] Notes made and supplied by M. Tanner.

[17] Churches Together in England 1997.

and, in a very helpful if self-effacing way, made available to the group his nearly fifty years of wider ecumenical experience, especially of the *BEM* process. Many of the issues, he felt, had already been discussed long enough. The real question was whether the churches would be prepared to act.[18]

A full picture of Morris West's ecumenical contribution should not, even in a sketch such as this, limit itself to a chronicle of the major events in which he was involved and to his recorded interventions and contributions. Many would say it was his singular style and presence which was so important. The minutes of the Plenary and Standing Commissions of Faith and Order mention him rarely, and indeed he spoke sparingly during such meetings. Yet those who worked with him leave no doubt that he was a significant and creative shaper of Faith and Order thinking, and in many respects more so than the habitually loquacious, the would-be pedagogues and sermonizers who are familiar enough on such occasions. When he did speak, it was in an effort to advance the discussion, to discern relationships and set in context, to reach a conclusion, and not just to stake out a position. Hence he was always listened to intently. Lukas Vischer recalls how at Loccum in 1977, Morris West set the terms of the whole morning's debate on baptism by his transparent commitment to see that all sides took the same fundamental questions seriously and honestly. In the corridors and at meal-tables, no less than in the small drafting groups where much of the real work is done, he was appreciated for his ability in helping people to say what they were wanting to express. And through it all came that wit - offhand, dry but never malicious. A German member of the WCC administrative staff still tells with affection how much she learned through him of the English art of blending humour with understatement.

In one further respect Morris West, to use Neville Clark's phrase, gave a nudge to history or at least laid a gentle finger upon it. Just as he himself had inherited the mantle from Ernest Payne, so in turn he enabled and encouraged certain younger people to enter the ecumenical scene. Mary Tanner, from 1991 to 1998 Moderator of Faith and Order, had her entrée into Faith and Order at Accra in 1974 as one of the 'Bristol gang', along with Morris West and the Methodists, Rupert Davies and Raymond George. She would, she confesses, have been totally overwhelmed without these mentors, especially Morris West who (in addition to advising her as they looked for their plane,

---

[18] Information supplied by M. Reardon.

'Trust in God and follow Rupert Davies') continually interpreted for her the sub-text within the official agenda of what was happening, and for the next twenty-five years remained her valued counsellor. Horace Russell of Jamaica, one of Morris West's students at Regent's Park, also became a Vice-Moderator of Faith and Order 1983-1991. Not only was it my own privilege, at his instigation, to follow Morris West into the Faith and Order Commission but the whole fifteen years experience of working closely with him in Bristol was one long induction into international ecumenical life. And one of the students in the last years of Morris West's Presidency at Bristol, Ruth Bottoms, is now both a member of the WCC Central Committee and Moderator of the WCC Commission on World Mission and Evangelism. Central to the West perception of the 'larger context' was that it includes time as well as space, and thus requires not only faithfulness to the past but also seed-sowing for the future.

Belief in the largest context of all, that of the overarching providence of God, was what enabled him to see that, properly viewed, everything has its 'normality' and therewith its true importance: the international, ecumenical scene and the local life of congregation or college. In both contexts, one should behave appropriately, neither with histrionics nor self-advertisement, nor evasion of proper responsibilities. Horatio in the end holds the stage. Or, if a more modest literary allusion is more acceptable, one may cite in conclusion the figure whom I once discovered to be another of Morris West's favourite characters, from W.E. Cule's *Sir Knight of the Splendid Way*.[19] Penned for evangelical youth in the 1930s, it reads like a re-write of *Pilgrim's Progress* by Walter Scott, as the young Sir Constant battles his way towards the City of the Great King, a way crossed with many a villain and hero. Morris West's favourite servant of the King, however, was not one of the knights who wrought great victories to public acclaim but the Warden of the Well, who would have loved to have been a knight himself but whose lifelong task (a 'reserved occupation'!) was to keep the water flowing pure from the spring which, streaming to far places, refreshed other pilgrims and adventurers on the way. Morris West did just that for the ecumenical movement, and the stream will flow for many a year to come.

KEITH CLEMENTS *General Secretary, Conference of European Churches*

---

[19] Religious Tract Society , n.d.

A FEW WORDS ABOUT THE CHRISTIAN MINISTRY
From the address by Dr West
at the ordination of Anthony R. Cross
18 March 1989 at New Road Baptist Church, Bromsgrove

Text: 2 Corinthians 5.17-6.10

In this passage Paul is reflecting autobiographically about the ministry. That is, about how things were going for him in the ministry. It is a passage, therefore, that is full of realism. There is no pretence about this, no false optimism, nor false pessimism. There is nothing unreal about it. Indeed, anybody who had the church at Corinth as part of his ministerial responsibility was bound to be a realist about the ministry.

In this passage Paul first of all lays down the foundation of the ministry, then talks about the lifestyle of the ministry and demands of the ministry. On the foundation of the ministry Paul is very clear. It all begins because the minister is and remains a converted person, a newly created person: 'Anyone in Christ is a new creation'. Therefore the conversion of the minister and, what is more, the sustaining of the conversion of the minister throughout his ministry is part of the foundation. A minister is in a particular sense a recreated person, who will go back time and again to the source of the conversion, Jesus Christ. The ministry is based upon Jesus Christ, not simply as a figure in history but as the Son of God and Saviour and Lord of the life of that individual. Only when the minister is and remains a converted person in that sense will the ministry sustain itself on the foundation which is intended by God.

That is obvious, but I need to say it at the beginning because in the ministry you need to go back. Paul is for ever going back and re-walking the Damascus Road. We may not all have a Damascus Road experience but we will all have an experience of Christ which is personal. You relive that experience and you hold to that experience. The foundation is that there is conversion.

The second foundation stone, as it were, in the ministry, as Paul makes very clear, is that there is a sense of God having 'called' and 'given'. It is interesting the way in which Paul uses this verb. A minister is not only 'called', he is 'given'. God has *given* us. In verse 18, 'who, through Christ reconciled us to himself and *gave* us'. It is a gift from God. Paul was very clear about that and clear about the implications - because, what God has given, God does not take away. The giving of the ministry by God is the constant recollection that you are not only therefore given, but you were called and therefore given. That is why the occasion of ordination is important: it is the day upon which in the laying on of hands, by a company gathered under God, the minister is called. This has to be the holding point throughout the ministry; this can be affirmed even when things are difficult. Paul found this as a stabilizer in the storm, that he was a called man and a given man, given to the Gentiles, given to this great ministry. He was able to hold fast to God because he knew that God had first held fast to him and went on holding fast. One of the most remarkable things about Paul is this sense of conviction that the grace and gift of God will always be sufficient for his need. It never ceases to amaze me, reading the letter to the Philippians, where he writes to his beloved church at Philippi, almost certainly from a prison cell, very probably from a condemned cell from which he was going out to martyrdom. Yet he reminds the people of Philippi that the peace of God which passes all understanding has 'garrisoned' (that's a strong word) his heart and mind through all the years. That is all you need in ministry: converted, called and sent by God. There is the foundation.

What about lifestyle? Again Paul is clear. It is, first of all, to be a reconciler; that is, one who, being reconciled to God in Christ, becomes a reconciler. That means nothing unless we recognize that what Paul was seeking to do in his ministry was to reconcile men and women to God and therefore to each other. For Paul, the vertical dimension, as it were, of reconciling them to God in Christ was at the same time reconciling them to each other. What he was doing was miraculous. The church at Corinth was a church largely full of Gentiles, non-Jews. This former Jewish Rabbi, now a Christian, is making his reconciliation appeal to the Gentiles - and succeeding. The very fact that the Christian church at Corinth and elsewhere produced a fellowship, a reconciled fellowship, which not only embraced Jew and Gentile (miraculous enough!) but also embraced master and slave, man and woman. The fact that these were all reconciled to one another because they were reconciled to God was in that world a miracle. So we are all called upon through the ministry to be those who seek to reconcile men and women to God in order that they may be reconciled to one another. The world needs the evidence today of a community of the miracle of reconciliation, so that people can say, 'Here is the way of peace on earth'. Here is the only hope of peace on earth - through reconciliation. The lifestyle is one of reconciliation: within the local church, between the churches, in the world. No wonder the going is hard!

Secondly, the lifestyle is that of the ambassador. 'Entrusting to us the message of reconciliation ..... So we are ambassadors of Christ'. We are representatives of Christ, representing the gospel in the world. That is a high calling and very demanding. But you are not alone; there is a community, a fellowship of ministry. You stand in a succession of ambassadors of previous generations. This is important. We Baptists do not believe in the episcopal laying on of hands in the sense that there is something essential about that. What we believe is that as Anthony kneels there he is being set in a succession of ministry through those of us who are here and share in the laying on of hands. It is true to say that back here, from this church in Bromsgrove, there are about fifty generations of ambassadors back to Christ himself. You are, as it were, in that succession of ministry. Jesus gave over the responsibility as his ambassadors - witnesses was the word in Acts 1.8, that's what an ambassador is, a witness to Christ. There they were, the first generation. Here you are, about fifty or so people in between. You can trace it back whichever way you like, through me, through your minister, through Neil Hall [the Area Superintendent who was present], whichever way seems safer to you, but it goes back. It is important to recognize that it goes back, and to recognize that there is this sense of fellowship within the ministry of these ambassadors. You, and your fellow students who send greetings from ministry where they are, are part of a called, responsible group, set throughout all the world - ambassadors.

Part of the lifestyle is, of course, that the ambassador is authorized. I hope the friends from the receiving church will recognize that in a very real sense the minister is God's gift to that church. The church has called him, believing him to be not simply a student seeking a church but a God-sent minister, who will seek to make his appeal to you on behalf of God. That is what it says: 'ambassadors for Christ, God making his appeal through us' - through the ministry. The minister therefore speaks as the called, sent man of God. The voice that speaks, therefore, in a very real sense in the proclamation, speaks the word of God. The love that comes in the pastoral office is the love of God in Christ as he moves amongst you as pastor. The minister comes authorized to represent the love of God to you. It is nothing less than that. He comes into your situation of pastoral need to say, as it were, 'I come as God's representative, making my offer and appeal of love and compassion and concern.' There is no reason why he should be there, were it not for the calling and sending of God. Therefore there is always this sense, not of self-confidence, but of divine sending and divine confidence that you are therefore authorized.

Paul was also clear about another part of the lifestyle of the reconciler and the ambassador. That is the urgency of the gospel. There is an urgency in what the minister has to do. In the synagogue at Nazareth, when Jesus had read from the prophet Isaiah about the one who was to come and the anointed one, he gave the book back to the attendant and said, 'Today is this scripture fulfilled in your ears'. From then on it became urgent, for God was at work in the world in Jesus Christ. Notice what Paul says at the beginning of chapter 6: 'Behold, now is the acceptable time; behold, now is the day of salvation'. And when you have a moment or two, it is worth looking at the 'nows' of scripture. Jesus uses the word often, so does Paul. Now is the judgment of this world, says Jesus. For the minister, therefore, part of his lifestyle must be the sense of urgency. Tomorrow may be too late, because today is the day of salvation. This sense of urgency should be upon the minister, whether preaching or pastoring. 'I'll come tomorrow', may be all right for some professions but is not all right for the ministry. Today, today, today. An urgency reflected in the necessity to bring the gospel day in and day out to the people in proclamation and in life and in pastoral care. There is something about the lifestyle - the reconciler, the called one, authorized to proclaim, to pastor, *urgently*, for the gospel.

Then there are the demands. Realism - it is there in the scriptures. 'Commend ourselves in every way: great endurance, afflictions, hardships, calamities' - there are plenty of those in the Baptist ministry. I have never yet been beaten (well, not literal 'beatings'); imprisonments - it has come to some; tumults, labours, watching, hunger. ' for Christ's sake': that is another of Paul's expressions. 'Fools for Christ's sake' - ministers! Yes, you are scarred, you will be scarred - it is inevitable. 'I did not come to be served', Jesus said, 'I came to serve and I came to give my life a ransom for many'. There is the reminder of the cost of ministry. The realism of Paul reminds us that the road ahead, the road we have promised to go with Jesus, and he has promised to go with you, will be from time to time a road where the going is rough, where you will bear scars. 'If anyone will come after me, let him deny himself and take up his cross and follow'. It is not the mini cross that he is talking about, it is the reality of the scars that he in the end uniquely and as a redeemer bore for us in his actual hands and side. This business of scars is part and parcel of our Christian understanding of the ministry.

John Bunyan (who, in spite of what anybody else says, was a Baptist) wrote in *Pilgrim's Progress* of Valiant for Truth. As he gets to the end of ministry, Valiant for Truth says, 'My sword I give to him that shall succeed me in my pilgrimage, and my courage and skill to him that can get it, but my marks and scars I carry with me to be a witness for me before him, that I fought his battles'.

The scars of the ministry are the signs of the faithful minister. You will accept them and you will receive them and, please God, you will bear them, not always bravely - because none of us are always brave - but as best you can, knowing that God is with you and remembering the end of all these quotations: 'Take up the cross and follow. Whoever gives up his life for my sake and the gospel's will find it'. That is the great paradox of the Christian gospel and also the paradox of the Christian ministry: it is through the scars and through the sufferings and through the sacrifice that one really discovers what it is all about. That is why through baptism we are buried with Christ and rise again. Beyond the scars is the whole Christian understanding of life. That is exactly what Paul says autobiographically. We are treated as imposters. Unknown? Well, yes, 'yet well known; as dying, and behold we live; as punished, and yet not killed; as sorrowful, yet always rejoicing; as poor, yet making many rich', not in money but in the gospel. 'Silver and gold have I none, but what I have give I unto you', said Peter and John to that man at the Beautiful Gate; 'rise up and walk'. There it is. These last words of verse 10 sustain me, and part of this autobiography of Paul is mine as well, though in a very pale reflection of his 'as having nothing and yet possessing everything'.

That is the paradox of ministry. There is no life like it, and there is no other calling that in the end shows a lost world the way home. To that you have been called. Remember, not what I have said, but what the word of God, through the words of St Paul, has tried to say to us today: hold fast to that as you hold fast to Christ, and you will find that you may not have too much as the world judges it, but in fact you have everything to give and in the ministry you will find that you receive more blessing than you ever dreamed was possible, far beyond one's deserving. God bless you and bless us all.

BAPTISTS TOGETHER
The Secretariat of the Baptist Union and effective denominational action

1 - J.H. SHAKESPEARE

It can be argued that the most significant date for Baptists in the twentieth century was 28 September 1898, just fifteen months before the twentieth century began, the day that J.H. Shakespeare was appointed by the Baptist Assembly to the secretaryship of the Baptist Union. For the story of 'Baptists Together' in the twentieth century is that of living with the consequences of that appointment. For Shakespeare sought to create a Baptist 'Union', which involved the attempt to develop the 'institutionalized interdependence' of independent and missionary-orientated churches. Shakespeare faced the churches with the question of how to function interdependently without sacrificing independence on the 'altar' of the 'inter'. It was a challenge which created not only potential positives, as the subsequent hundred years have shown, but also divisive negatives. And the paradox was - and is - that some of those negatives are created by positive Baptist principles.

As the twenty-first century dawns, Baptists are still seeking to work out how to live together in an interdependence which will enable the challenges and opportunities of the new millennium to be met without denying that fundamental Baptist principle that 'each church has liberty under the guidance of the Holy Spirit to interpret and administer His laws'. This is an issue which affects every church in the Union and which determines the practical outworking of the life of the English Baptist family of churches. This 'reflection' is not intended as a 'potted history' of the Union; rather it is concerned to trace its practical networking as churches, colleges and associations sought to understand what in the modern world it meant to be 'Baptists Together'.

J.H. Shakespeare was born on 10 April 1857. His grandfather and his father were Baptist pastors. Shakespeare was a deeply committed Baptist by upbringing. Writing in 1918 he commented, 'Since I grew to man's estate, I have revisited the little Chapel in the lovely village where my grandfather ministered "on forty pounds a year". I am conscious that what is good in me came from that humble meeting house'. His father was the pastor of the Baptist church in Malton, a North Yorkshire town on the road from York to Scarborough. As his obituarist, Charles Brown, wrote in the *Baptist*

Handbook, 'It seems to many people a serious misfortune that any biography of him is forbidden by his own wish, one would have loved to know something about his boyhood, and whether then there was promise of the brilliant achievements of his manhood'.

We know, however, that he worked briefly in an insurance office in London and that from earliest days he had sensed a ministerial calling. While in London he became a member of the Regent's Park Chapel, a thriving church under the effective ministry of Dr Landels. In 1878 Shakespeare was accepted by Regent's Park College and in 1883, having obtained an MA Honours Degree from London University, he was called, at the age of twenty-six, to the pastorate of St Mary's, Norwich, a significant church of 235 members. When Shakespeare left Norwich in 1898 the membership had doubled to 479.

In 1892 he made his first appearance on the platform of the Baptist Union Assembly. At the Baptist Union Council the previous October, he had moved a resolution to the effect that the already existing Home Mission Fund should take over the responsibility for a church extension initiative, particularly in those urban areas where there was no Baptist church. John Clifford seconded the proposal and the Council agreed that a plan should be prepared. As the proposer of the resolution Shakespeare was asked to undertake this in time for the 1892 Union Assembly. Shakespeare presented his plan to the morning session of the Assembly on Thursday, 28 April, in the Bloomsbury Chapel. The title was *Baptist Church Extension in Large Towns*. It was a remarkable and challenging utterance, calling for a nationwide scheme for urban church extension. It was surely not coincidental that the Scripture which preceded Shakespeare's address was Revelation 3: 7-13, a word directed to the church at Philadelphia, with its clarion call: 'I know what you are doing, I have set before you an open door which no one can shut'.

In retrospect, this address by Shakespeare can be seen to be more than a call to church extension made by a young and enthusiastic Baptist minister. It contained within it Shakespeare's conviction as to the theological concept upon which the Union should be based. It verged on a manifesto for the Baptist denomination.

He began by stating that his purpose was to produce not only a plan for a denominational extension but that the proposed scheme: 'was an attempt to weld into a real and active unity the scattered or contending forces of the Baptist Churches of Great Britain'. He argued that the present lack of system had produced a mistaken policy. His proposals, he claimed, were for a scheme which 'is not connexional or Presbyterian, but entirely in harmony with a wise and sympathetic congregationalism'. Associations such as London and Yorkshire had undertaken Church Extension. What was now needed was a Baptist Union Extension Fund to receive collections, subscriptions and legacies and which would take a wide survey of the need. Such a survey would be aware of other denominations. Shakespeare nailed what we would call his 'ecumenical colours' to the mast. 'We desire to accept and we appeal to the Congregationalists and Wesleyans to accept the spirit of the recent resolutions of the Three Denominations that in undertaking new work we regard churches and stations existing and connected with the Free Evangelical Churches as if they were our own'.

To his fellow Baptists, Shakespeare did not mince his words. The thirty-five year old enthusiast fearlessly challenged the *status quo.*

> I am aware that one great obstacle to this movement will be the chilling indifference with which many regard any proposals for Church Extension. Some of us do not care a straw whether a large town contains one or fifty Baptist chapels so long as our own is prospering. Others, however, will offer a direct opposition based on party cries, empty quibbles and dismal echoes of principles they have never grasped. They will talk of unorganized Congregationalism, of endowments and of individual efforts. Unorganized Congregationalism is to-day only another name for selfishness. Is it right to meet the religious destitution of the masses by a split or a lucky accident, and wrong to meet it by a systematic and generous movement?

Shakespeare goes on to proclaim himself an ardent supporter of Voluntaryism but not of unorganized Voluntaryism. Contemporary challenges require united action.

> The fathers of Independency maintained an unbroken front against king and prelate ..... We need such a movement as this for the ennobling of the Baptist Union itself ..... Yet have we not sometimes stood like a life-boat crew engaged in angry debate upon the shore, heedless of the cries for help borne to us across the waves?

As his oratory reaches its climax the metaphor changes from drowning mariners to starving multitudes:

> But brethren, the famine of which we speak is a spiritual one; we are

> stewards of the bread of life - during the last decade three millions have been added to the population of England alone. Multitudes have died in spiritual darkness ….. God forgive us that we have been in the midst of the perishing multitudes not like the compassionate Master, but enjoying our religious privileges, rapt in glorious memories and clutching at a dead idol, the brazen and deceptive serpent of an extreme and selfish independency.

The Assembly accepted the scheme!

His address was soon published in its entirety. His hearers and his readers can have been in no doubt but that here was a voice challenging the Baptist *status quo* with prophetic vehemence and conviction. Yet it was to the possessor of this voice that the Baptist Council and Assembly turned when it became clear that the health of the Secretary of the Baptist Union, Samuel Harris Booth, was failing.

At the Spring Assembly of 1898 the President, Samuel Vincent of George Street, Plymouth, reported on steps taken with a view to nominating a successor to Booth. The name which the Nomination Committee, on behalf of the Council, had intended to bring to the Assembly was that of J.H. Shakespeare, who had consented to such nomination. The *Baptist Magazine* of May 1898 spoke of 'general satisfaction' being felt at the announcement, and went on to remark, 'Mr Shakespeare possesses qualities which have made him an able and efficient administrator and an eloquent representative of the Union in all public functions. He has both "culture and go". He is clear-sighted, bold in conception with a well balanced judgement and something of the daring of genius. He has the power of initiation and something of the energy of enthusiasm.'

But there was a snag. The resolution moved on behalf of the Council was not immediately to appoint Shakespeare but rather, 'That the election of a Secretary be deferred until the Autumn Assembly and that the Council are hereby instructed to take the necessary steps in the meantime to secure a suitable nomination and to provide for carrying on the work of the office'. The comment in the *Baptist Magazine* continues:

> It is, therefore, with profound regret that we hear of the enforced withdrawal of his nomination in consequence of a serious, though it is hoped, temporary, failure of his health. Three medical advisers insist upon this withdrawal and it is evidently a necessity. It is by no means improbable that this breakdown is due to the severe strain of Mr Shakespeare's efforts in connection with the Church Extension

Scheme which, in addition to his pastoral work, have overtaxed his strength.'

It cannot have helped that by 1898 only about £10,000 had been collected of the hoped for £100,000 when the Church Extension Scheme was launched six years earlier.

This tendency to depression - for that is what this breakdown seems to have been - as Shakespeare's son Geoffrey subsequently revealed - was to be a recurrent factor in Shakespeare's life. It is a tendency which can be temperamentally inherent in those who live very much on their nerves - but as a result possess also the daring of genius and the energy of enthusiasm. Nervous energy is often the source of such genius and enthusiasm.

Fortunately, Shakepeare's 'attacks' were relatively short-lived and by the autumn of 1898 he had recovered. On 28 September 1898 the resolution for his election was moved at the Autumn Assembly of the Union at Nottingham by Samuel Vincent, supported by two influential laymen, one being W.R. Rickett JP of London, 'and carried with hearty enthusiasm. The audience rose to its feet when Mr Shakespeare came on to the platform'.

The *Baptist Magazine* for November 1898 commented: 'In view of his improved health, the election was, indeed, a foregone conclusion - one to which the denomination at large had evidently made up its mind; indeed, so strong was the feeling that the Secretarial Committee felt that no other course was even open for consideration'.

At the Assembly W.R. Rickett described Shakespeare as 'a man of energy and power and the work that he had done in the past has an assurance of what he was capable of doing in the future ..... He was a man of great enthusiasm and zeal'. The events that followed so swiftly on Shakespeare's election confirm that the tributes paid to him were not exaggerated. In essence, Shakespeare set himself the task of creating a Baptist Union expressive of institutionalized interdependence out of the raw material of independent, diverse and missionary-minded churches. The story of Baptists Together in the twentieth century is that of living with the consequences of his attempt to create an effective vehicle for vibrant denominational life with all its potential positives and recurring negatives. His first main objective during his term of office was the launching and carrying through of the Twentieth Century Fund. Within twelve hours of his election that Fund was already on its way towards its launch!

Shakespeare attributed the germ of the idea for the Fund to Samuel Vincent, the Union President in 1898-99. In a casual conversation after a meeting of the nominations sub-committee early in September 1898, Vincent, Shakespeare and Charles Williams of Accrington were in a committee room in the Mission House in Furnival Street where the Union had its office. Vincent posed the question whether the Baptists could raise a great Fund as the Wesleyans were doing to celebrate the dawn of the new century. 'Why cannot we erect a Baptist House to be the Headquarters of the Baptist Union?' Apparently the three of them agreed that Vincent would make this suggestion in his address, as President, to the Autumn Assembly at Nottingham later that month. True to his word, on 28 September, in his address which followed immediately after Shakespeare's election, Vincent said:

> As a denomination we lodge in the Mission House, and have no house of our own in the metropolis of the world. Would it be no advantage to our great and growing spiritual work, to our units and our extension, to have a building that might house many, if not all, our Baptist Societies under one roof? ..... Till we get such a house - which we reasonably hope may not be too long - there may be a doubt of its worth to us. Ten years after we get it, we shall be amused, if not amazed, that we were content to lodge in three or four rooms in the Mission House, that friendliest house in the world.

But Vincent was not content with that suggestion! He regretted that the Extension Fund had not reached one-tenth of the hoped-for hundred thousand pounds and then went on, quite remarkably, to suggest that British Baptists should set out to raise at least £200,000 'to replenish approved funds and to extend our work in all the needed places'.

According to Shakespeare's subsequent account of the proceedings at Nottingham, 'These bold and far reaching suggestions were received almost in silence by an Assembly which scarcely knew whether to regard the proposals as practical or as visionary and quixotic'. The *Baptist Magazine* for November simply commented: 'The part of the address that will receive most comment was the closing suggestion as to the building of a Church House in London where all our Societies could be accommodated under one roof and the raising of a fund of £200,000 for aggressive purposes'. On the face of it, probably Shakespeare's word 'quixotic' was the most accurate description of how the delegates would view this suggestion. The denomination had already proper and regular demands on the purses of local churches through the Home Mission, Augmentation and Church Extension Funds. Now it was suggested that an attempt should be made to raise upwards of £200,000. In 1898 £250,000 would be the equivalent of raising £13.75 million in 1999. If this was not tilting at a windmill, what was?

Vincent, in his address, judiciously reminded the delegates that it was at Nottingham that Carey preached his so-called 'deathless' sermon with the refrain of expecting great things from God and of attempting great things for God. He did not claim exact parallels but left the delegates to work it out for themselves.

It is evident that Shakespeare was possessed of the 'power of initiation' and 'energy of enthusiasm'. On the morning of 28 September he had been elected as Secretary of the Baptist Union. His election was followed by a Presidential utterance calling for plans basically to re-found the Baptist Union structurally in bricks and mortar, in financial potential and in the creation of a greater number of departments to serve the Baptist denomination. At 5.15 p.m. the same day the General Purposes Committee met, ostensibly to fulfil the request of the previous day's Council to prepare a programme for the Spring Assembly in 1899. In fact, the General Purposes Committee used that remit to appoint a sub-committee consisting of the officers, together with the Revds J.C. Carlile, E.G. Gange, C. Williams and J.R. Wood: 'to consider any scheme desirable to be submitted in regard to the "Century Fund" contemplated in the President's Address and report such scheme to this committee for the next meeting of the Council with a view to a Public Meeting on Monday evening, 24th April 1899'. So within eight hours of Shakespeare's appointment the Twentieth Century Fund Scheme was well on its way towards presentation to the Spring Assembly of 1899. That night the new Secretary must have slept the sleep of the well satisfied enthusiast!

The time schedule set out in the resolution of the General Purposes Committee of 28 September was adhered to exactly. A Baptist Union Council was held on 18 January 1899, attended by some eighty members - a good attendance by late nineteenth-century standards. There were nearly forty letters of apology, two of which, from Drs Angus and Brown, were read, and these together with most of the others 'expressed sympathy with the proposal to raise a "Twentieth Century Fund"'. A draft scheme for such a Fund was presented. This scheme had been prepared by the group set up by the General Purposes Committee on the previous 28 September. It had been discussed at three subsequent meetings of that committee. Shakespeare moved and T.M. Harris seconded the reception of the Report for discussion by Council. The determinative minute records that the scheme 'was moved in detail from the Chair (S. Vincent), seconded by J.R. Wood, and after prolonged discussion unanimously and enthusiastically adopted as amended'.

The main purpose of the Fund was to enhance the means whereby Baptists could 'defend, advocate and preserve in our country the simple Gospel of Jesus Christ'. The amount to be raised was £250,000 from 500,000 Baptists. Half the Fund would be allocated to the 'evangelisation of our country and Church Extension'. The other half was to be applied to a number of purposes, including the erection of a Baptist Church House, assistance with the maintenance of pastors, and the Annuity Fund for aged ministers and the widows of ministers.

At the Spring Assembly the general principle of such a fund was accepted as part of the Council's Report given on Monday, 24 April 1900. A mass rally was held in the City Temple the same evening. The recently founded *Baptist Times and Freeman* described this as 'an immense gathering ..... which completely filled the building ..... and the meeting throughout was marked by a high degree of enthusiasm'. Association Secretaries and Treasurers were entertained at breakfast at the Holborn Restaurant on Tuesday, 25 April, and the following day leading laymen were given lunch at the same venue. On Thursday, 27 April, details of the proposed Fund were presented to the Assembly, at which, so the *Baptist Times* reported, 'a larger number of ministers and delegates were present than had ever attended the Spring meetings of the Union on any previous occasion'. After discussion, clarification and amendment the Scheme was adopted.

Shakespeare, in 1904, published a detailed account of the raising of the Fund. He included stories of mass rallies addressed by great denominational leaders, notably A.C. Maclaren, John Clifford and himself. To read again the verbatim reports of their speeches is to hear the last orators of a past age. Their passion encouraged remarkable response. More than seventy Association and District organizers were appointed and they helped to stimulate the appointment of representatives of the Fund in each local church. The women of the denomination organized a 'Baptist Women's Shilling Fund' (a shilling was worth then nearly £5 of today's money) and collected nearly 800,000 shillings (£40,000).

The pages of the *Baptist Times and Freeman* were full of accounts of such gatherings and recorded the progress of the Fund. This was not surprising as the purchase of the *Freeman*, which was a privately owned Baptist publication and its combination with the new *Baptist Times*, founded in February 1899, had been one of the first actions which Shakespeare took as Secretary of the Union. He had a large share of its editorial direction, helped by his brother Alfred. It proved a valuable propaganda asset in the raising of the Fund and, more generally, of keeping the churches informed, nurturing them into a larger vision of the church and eliciting their support and involvement in issues beyond the immediate concerns of the local congregation - not that all rose to that challenge or cared about the larger issues. Apathy as much as opposition faced Shakespeare's vision of a Union of churches effectively interdependent for the purposes of mission and extension.

The Fund was to close on Thursday, 1 May 1902, the last day of the Spring Assembly. By the Monday, 28 April, the total was £241,000. By the Wednesday it had reached £244,674. The drama continued to the last. Shakespeare records what happened:

> On the Wednesday afternoon (30 April) a hansom cab drove up to the Mission House and from it alighted the two friends Mr and Mrs John Chivers ..... Mr Chivers informed me that £5,000[1] would be given by the family and one or two friends in memory of his brother, Mr William Chivers JP.

So £326 remained to be found. Shakespeare telegraphed the news to John Marnham and Edward Robinson, who agreed to find this balance. Thus on Thursday morning, 1 May, Shakespeare could announce the completion of the Fund. Not surprisingly, the Assembly spontaneously responded by standing to sing the Doxology. The completion of the Fund was a great achievement for Baptists not accustomed to working together on such a scale for mission at home. Around Shakespeare in this task were men like John Clifford, Henry Wood, Alexander McLaren, William Cuff, J.A. Spurgeon, J.W. Ewing, Herbert Marnham, D.J. Hiley and Richard Glover - all men of independent mind prepared to work together for the good of interdependent Baptist witness.

By any standards, the raising of this Fund was an astonishing achievement by the Baptists at the turn of the twentieth century. It was all the more so because, whilst Baptists had been so engaged, the soldiers of the Queen had been marching through the City streets *en route* to South Africa and the Boer War. It was not until just after the completion of the Fund that that weary and somewhat controversial war dragged finally to its end. In addition, the Victorian era had literally come to its end with the death of the Queen in January 1901. She was the only monarch that the vast majority of the population had ever known. Reclusive and distant she may have been in

---

[1] This would be some £250,000 in 1999 currency.

her latter years but she was more than a figurehead of stability and confidence.

The same year that saw the Fund's completion also saw the foundation stone laid for the Baptist Church House in Southampton Row. In 1903 the new House was opened and Shakespeare set to work to develop the structures of interdependence there. Knowing the importance of 'communication' he had, in 1902, initiated a Publications Department which in the following year opened a bookshop in the new Church House. A Young People's Union was formed in 1904 to which youth societies of the local churches could affiliate. In 1905 a Baptist Insurance Company was formed, and the work of the Baptist Total Abstinence Union was encouraged, with the fast developing Bands of Hope which older readers may recall with mixed memories! Very importantly, in 1908 the Baptist Women's Home Work Auxiliary was formed. As we have seen, there was an effective *ad hoc* group of women which helped in the raising of the Twentieth Century Fund; now the women's work quickly became an effective part of the work of the Union, changing its name in 1910 to the Baptist Women's League. Shakespeare was concerned to consolidate the various Funds of the Union, helped by the financial boost from the Twentieth Century Fund. By 1905 the Home Work Fund was in being, incorporating the Home Mission, the Church Extension and the Augmentation Funds.

Shakespeare was determined to move still further along the path of interdependence. Others shared with him the desire to develop a Sustentation Fund which involved fixing a minimum salary for ministers and also aiding churches centrally to maintain such a stipend. This in turn would lead to ministerial recognition and a system of help for churches and ministers in the settlement processes. Many saw, however, that this might be a serious infringement upon the independence of the local church. For his part Shakespeare believed that prophetic leadership had to challenge anything that smacked of congregational isolationism, and if that involved a measure of institutional centralization then that was a price that had to be paid and opposition had to be firmly countered.[2]

There was considerable and influential opposition, notably from Richard Glover of Bristol and Moffat Logan of Accrington. Both these ministers had come from presbyterian backgrounds and felt perhaps more strongly than

---

[2] The long and complex story of the bringing into being in 1912 of the Ministerial Settlement and Sustentation Scheme has been told already in detail by Douglas C. Sparkes, *An Accredited Ministry*, Baptist Historical Society 1996.

others the dangers of institutional interdependence, but they did not win the day.

The acceptance of the Scheme in 1912 led to the introduction of General Superintendents in 1916 and the raising of a further £250,000 for the Sustentation Fund which was completed by 1917 - in the midst of a war far more significant and demanding than the earlier Boer War. It is likely that the success of the earlier Fund spurred Shakespeare on to try yet again to stabilize the funds of Baptist interdependence.

In all this activity Shakespeare was simply putting into practice the principles he had clearly enunciated to the Assembly in 1892 in connection with the Extension Fund. The opposition, who argued that what was happening was the 'clericalizing' and 'professionalizing' of the ministry, as well as the serious infringement of the true Baptist nature of the local church, with its 'liberty to interpret and administer the laws of Christ as contained in the Holy Scripture', had been for the moment outvoted. But the debate about interdependence did not and would not go away throughout the whole of the century. It continues still as a twentieth-century legacy to the next century.

By 1912, however, the Baptists as a national denomination could 'walk tall'. The future seemed set fair. Financially stabilization was the plan; structurally there was a headquarters with an enthusiastic and determined General Secretary and a growing organization of the scattered forces into an effective Gospel army.

Yet, at the same time, there were concerns. The known membership of churches in fellowship with the Baptist Union peaked in 1906 with 410,766 members and just under 570,000 Sunday School scholars in 2,811 churches. Thereafter membership figures began to fall. As early as 1908 Shakespeare was talking about 'the arrested progress of the Church'. Had this anything to do with the developing interdependence of the Baptists? Views were expressed, though no-one could be quite certain one way or the other. It is a question which today still remains unanswered.

Shakespeare was not simply concerned with the development of the Baptist Union. He was a man of many enthusiasms, including the wider Church community. Globally he shared with Baptists of other countries the vision of a world gathering of Baptists. John Rippon in 1790 had dreamed of drawing together in London Baptists from other parts of the world. In 1904 this idea was revived in the United States by Dr Prestridge and taken up by Shakespeare. The result was that the Baptist Union Council issued an invitation to Baptists world-wide to attend a Congress in London in 1905. That July, Baptist representatives from twenty-three countries met in the

Exeter Hall in London. On 17 July they agreed to form a Baptist World Alliance, with John Clifford as first President and Shakespeare and Prestridge as joint Secretaries. This began to lead in turn to closer contact amongst European Baptists.[3]

It was not only with other Baptists that Shakespeare's enthusiasm demanded he should have fellowship: it was also with Christians of other Churches. He was an ecumenical enthusiast and it was his pursuit of the elusive ecumenical ideal that caused him even greater problems within his own denomination than did his strenuous development of Baptist interdependence. This ecumenical issue was to run and run within the Baptist Union throughout much of the twentieth century.

The publication in 1918 of *The Churches at the Cross Roads*, which may be called Shakespeare's *apologia pro vita sua* and his ecumenical confession of faith, was for many of his Baptist colleagues, indeed probably for the majority, a step too far. Whilst the loyalty of his influential colleagues in the Baptist Union Council was assured, and they were supportive of his work of restructuring the Union, more and more of his friends had, on the ecumenical issue, to become his defenders rather than fellow advocates of policy. Shakespeare realized this and felt himself after 1918 growingly isolated.

In the final years of his Secretaryship he was, however, successful in working with the BMS in 1920 in the raising of yet another £250,000.[4] Most of the Union's half-share in this Fund was given to the Sustentation Fund in support of ministerial stipends.

Shakespeare's fragile health was being adversely affected by the stresses created by the passionate and fearless advocacy of his own convictions. In 1921 he broke down again and, in spite of a brief recovery in 1923, he collapsed both mentally and physically. He resigned at the Assembly of 1924 and died on 12 March 1928.

Much of what follows in the story of the twentieth century will reflect, one way or another, upon Shakespeare's legacy to English Baptist life throughout the century. He was fortunate in the stature of the Baptist leaders around him, both ministerial and lay. A.C. Maclaren, Samuel Vincent, F.B. Meyer, John Clifford, Richard Glover, J.C. Carlile, Charles Williams, Herbert Marnham, Henry Wood, Edward Robinson, T.S. Penny, to name but a few. They were men of substance both spiritually and, in many of the lay, materially as well.

---

[3] See Bernard Green, *Crossing the Boundaries: a history of the European Baptist Federation*, 1999.

[4] By this time the pound would be worth some £21 of today's money

Their gifts were offered to their generation of Baptists and they ensured the establishment of the Baptist Union as envisaged by Shakespeare. In a proper sense, they gave Shakespeare his head and accepted that there would be times when they would need to pull sharply on the reins - sometimes in vain. But they were a relatively small group - almost an oligarchy, with a small cabal effectively in charge of Union affairs.

Although Shakespeare's achievements were substantial and his legacy significant, the evidence does not suggest that acceptance of the concept of a Baptist Union and its support became a significant and lasting high priority for the local churches in the first two decades of the twentieth century. It is true that the Twentieth Century Fund was completed - and other subsequent appeals. But there is not strong evidence to suggest that the churches up and down the land 'owned' and shared consciously in the Union in interdependence. The churches - especially the ministers - were glad of the benefits that came their way, but they had other and to them higher priorities on their minds, notably their independent survival through constant evangelism and mission in a century which began so confidently but was within fourteen years rudely and violently shaken by the First World War. The Baptist Union Council itself, which had a potential membership at the turn of the century of 160 drawn from all over the country, rarely had an attendance of more than seventy, and often far fewer. Of course, means of transport were more limited then, yet greater enthusiasm for the Union would surely have been reflected in larger attendances. Oral tradition suggests also that there were signs already of the 'them and us' culture towards the Union so far as local churches were concerned, a culture that tended to become more prevalent as the century progressed.

Shakespeare's concept of the Union was, however, here to stay. This mounted a challenge to belong to one another and offered the local churches opportunities to benefit. It was destined also to be the focus of continuing debate, discussion and argument for the next hundred years.

2 - M.E. AUBREY

On 28 April 1925 at the Baptist Union Assembly in Bloomsbury Shakespeare's successor was appointed. The President of the Union, Mr T.S. Penny of Taunton, proposed the election of Melbourn Evans Aubrey as General Secretary. Herbert Marnham, the Union Treasurer who had been in office since 1900, seconded. The resolution was carried unanimously. The *Baptist Times* of 1 May described the scene.

> Mr Aubrey was welcomed by the President, who held him by the hand for quite a few moments. The feeling of some of our leaders was apparent in eyes that glistened strangely. It could not but be felt by them that a new chapter in our denominational life was being opened in that welcoming act. An old order was passing, grand but now closed. A new era was coming to birth.

In the gallery at Bloomsbury that day sat a young student at Regent's Park College: Ernest Payne wondered whether things would turn out quite like that! Thirty-two years later it fell to that same Ernest Payne to write the *Baptist Union Handbook* memoir of Aubrey. He concluded by saying that during his all too brief retirement Aubrey had been able to look back with satisfaction on the consolidation and expansion of the work of the Union 'during a period of unusual difficulty'.

This is an accurate description of Aubrey's years in office. When he was elected in 1925, the immediate post-war hopes of the 'land fit for heroes to live in' had faded. His first Assembly in Leeds in 1926 coincided with the General Strike, which was incidentally amongst the earlier events to have left an indelible memory in the present writer's mind. There followed years of economic depression and social unrest. Unemployment was rife and poverty common. Childhood memories of urban life abound with ex-servicemen begging in streets or standing in an *ad hoc* group in the gutters, trying to play musical instruments in tune to earn 'a copper to feed the kids'.

In the early 1930s Hitler began his rise to power and the nations moved, as we can see now, inexorably towards a second world war. Organized religion was in decline and Baptists were not exempt. The Baptist Union itself and many local Baptist churches were experiencing a period of challenge and uncertainty. Michael Goodman described it as a 'long term deepening crisis of confidence and identity'.[5] In retrospect, that may well be true, yet at the time, Baptist life was far from being 'all down and glum'.

In 1939 war came again. During the war years and the six years after the war before he retired, Aubrey's true leadership qualities showed themselves. Aubrey's time in office was far from easy, yet the influence of Baptists together functioning as the Union became more and more evident, whether all local churches liked it or not!

Aubrey was a Welshman, born on 21 April 1885, during his father's ministry at Zion, Pentre. He was the eldest of a family of six. In 1899 he was sent as a boarder to Taunton School where he excelled academically and became head boy. He sensed a call to ministry and entered South Wales Baptist College in 1904, where he graduated through the University College of South Wales and Monmouthshire. In 1908, together with a Rawdon student named Arthur Dakin, he benefited from the Twentieth Century Fund by being awarded a Baptist Union Scholarship. Dakin went to Halle and Heidelberg; Aubrey, after abortive correspondence with Union Theological Seminary in New York, went to Mansfield College, Oxford, where he became a close friend of a fellow student, a Congregationalist scholar, Charles H. Dodd. During his final year, his parents, together with all his brothers and sisters, emigrated to America. He graduated from Oxford in 1911 and settled as Associate Minister at Victoria Road, Leicester. He found the church exciting and forward-looking, with a warm and welcoming fellowship. He was active pastorally and showed an evident competence as a preacher.

News of his ability spread. Within a year, however, in those days before the advent of General Superintendents, he was 'head-hunted' by T.R. Glover on behalf of St Andrew's Street, Cambridge. Aubrey was reluctant to move so quickly but pressure upon him grew. Letters arrived from J.H. Shakespeare, W.Y. Fullerton, Secretary of the Baptist Missionary Society, and J.W. Ewing, President of the Baptist Union, to name but a few. All sought to persuade him to go to Cambridge. It is an extraordinary example of the denominational 'free for all' which existed in the absence of any settlement system. Glover argued, 'If it were any other church you might stay where you are. But you can do what is needed in Cambridge and Cambridge calls you'.

A unanimous call was issued by the church meeting and backed up by a formidable delegation which visited the Aubrey home in Leicester. The

---

[5] Michael Goodman, 'English and Welsh Baptists in the 1930s', doctoral dissertation, Open University, 1993.

Principal of Mansfield joined in with a persuasive letter, so Aubrey moved to Cambridge in February 1913 and stayed at St Andrew's Street for twelve years. By any standards, humanly speaking, the Cambridge ministry was successful. The church grew numerically from 412 members in 1913 to 544 in 1925. This was against the stream of denominational decline. Aubrey was an outstanding preacher and pastor. He was happy and influential in Cambridge, both in city and university. But in 1925, by a strange irony (presumably divine!) he was to be 'head-hunted' yet again by T.R. Glover, one of his own deacons, on behalf of the Baptist Union.

When Shakespeare resigned because of ill health in 1924, J.C. Carlile, the minister of Folkestone and editor of the *Baptist Times*, agreed to act as secretary for a year. During the summer of 1924 Carlile indicated that he was unlikely to accept the position permanently. On 18 November the Baptist Union Council set up a Nominations Committee, consisting of the officers of the Union, together with fifteen representatives from around the country. To this group were added two representatives of the Baptist Women's League. It may say something of Baptist ways of doing things in those days, if we record that T.R. Glover's diary for 1 November reads:

> Council sets up Committee to propose name of new Secretary - who will be Aubrey, now Rushbrooke clear that he will stick to the European work.

When the Selection Committee met on 19 December with T.R. Glover, President of the Union, in the chair, he did, indeed, open proceedings by reading two letters, one from Carlile and the other from Rushbrooke, each requesting that their names should not be considered. Rushbrooke in 1924 was functioning on behalf of the Baptist World Alliance as full-time Commissioner co-ordinating European work and acting as a Baptist ambassador within Europe.

No detail is given of the protracted discussion which followed the reading of these letters. The minutes simply record that one name was agreed upon for recommendation to the Council on 20 January 1925. The name was to remain strictly confidential. It seems, however, that Aubrey was informed, also in confidence, that he was to be the sole nominee. Unfortunately 'confidentiality' proved to be, as so often, an impossibility in practice and there was a 'leak' into the infamous ecclesiastical grapevine. The *Christian World* of 25 December carried two paragraphs on the Baptist succession: one to the effect that Dr Carlile was not a candidate for the vacant Secretaryship;

the other, under the heading of 'Probable Secretary', read:

> The name of Rev. M.E. Aubrey of Cambridge is freely [!] mentioned as the probable successor to Dr J.H. Shakespeare as Secretary of the Baptist Union now that Dr Carlile has intimated his desire to retain his Folkestone pastorate.

When Aubrey read these reports he was, not unnaturally, deeply concerned. He did not want to leave Cambridge and he had evidence enough to be certain that St Andrew's Street would not want him to leave. He was unable to talk openly with his deacons, for *he* respected the word 'confidential'. Now it was being hinted that he was a second (or even third) choice for the nomination.

Influential Baptist leaders wrote to Aubrey, reassuring him of their support. But Aubrey wrote to Glover, as chairman of the nominating committee, refusing to let his name go to the Baptist Union Council later in January after all. This produced a further crop of letters, seeking to persuade him to allow the nomination to proceed. A meeting was arranged between Glover, Marnham, Charles Brown and Aubrey. This was far from easy but the outcome was that Aubrey withdrew his objections and allowed his name to go to Council. There his nomination was moved by Glover, who made it clear that neither Carlile nor Rushbrooke were candidates, and seconded by Rushbrooke himself. A number of speakers, representing different denominational interests as well as different geographical areas, spoke warmly in favour. The outcome was inevitable. When Aubrey returned to Council all the members rose in their places to signify unanimous support. Aubrey thanked them and said he would now consult the church at Cambridge. He added, somewhat enigmatically, that he believed that a man who left a church and a pastorate took a step downward. Council agreed to write to St Andrew's Street, explaining the nature, strength and reason for the invitation.

There is extant a remarkable and verbatim account of the church meeting at St Andrew's Street, in the course of which one member described Glover as 'a predatory hawk with the spirit of a dove'! This meeting, held on 28 January 1925, shows a Baptist church meeting at its spiritual best. Many speakers participated, about twenty in all. The resolution before the meeting spoke of the honour shown in such a call to the secretaryship; the effectiveness of Aubrey and recognition of his ministry; and the principle that 'the denomination as a whole should be considered before the interests of any particular church', while arguing that both had to exist for the extension of the Kingdom of God. Finally, the meeting expressed confidence that the minister would consider prayerfully and carefully whether the Kingdom might not be better served by his remaining in Cambridge, and assured Aubrey of the confidence, esteem and prayers of his people as he considered what to do. On 7 February Aubrey wrote accepting nomination and he was appointed formally by the Assembly on 28 April.

The purpose of recounting in some detail this episode of Aubrey's call to office is not simply to record but also to illustrate that during the twentieth century those called to the Secretaryship of the Union have not been those seeking power and authority for themselves, leaders seeking acclamation. Rather have they been those who, on the whole, have accepted with some reluctance, recognizing that such an office would be not only fulfilling but also demanding and costly.

Baptists collectively, like everybody else, are capable of great enthusiasm, possessing considerable powers of persuasion, and having good intentions of unswerving support in encouraging people to serve them. But, as one suspects every Union Secretary has found, memories can be short when hard and sometimes divisive options have to be placed before the denomination. Those of us who engage in retrospective writing need always to take care that a combination of hindsight and a failure to appreciate the contextual limitations which faced past decision-takers do not lead us into harsh and unfair judgements on those who have been called to serve the denomination in responsible positions. Baptist Union Secretaries can only be what everyone else can only be - themselves, serving with others under God and following what appears to them at the time to be divine purpose.

As it was with Shakespeare, so it was with Aubrey. He knew that the decisive actions of the past twenty-five years could not be reversed. The Union with its concept of interdependence was here to stay. But if Shakespeare had the gift of prophetic leadership, Aubrey recognized now the need for the gift of consolidation. This he possessed. His son, Peter, once commented that his father's main preoccupation was to become a *compositeur aimable*, a gracious peacemaker. For then, as now, the denominational interdependence of independent churches could be a fragile vessel.

In his last years Shakespeare's ecumenical enthusiasm had moved too far and too fast for many Baptists. The mind of the denomination on ecumenism was somewhat uncertain, particularly as a result of the Conversations on Church Union which had followed the Lambeth Appeal of 1920. It is unlikely to be coincidental that Aubrey's first Assembly, when the President was none other than J.H. Rushbrooke, should be an occasion for 'beating the Baptist drum'. The Assembly theme was 'The Faith of the Baptists'.

But Aubrey in his own way proved to be a quiet but determined ecumenist. He became involved in the work of Faith and Order and of Life and Work. He encouraged the participation of others and, in due course, was himself a member of the committee of fourteen which, just prior to the Second World War, planned the basis of the World Council of Churches. Indeed, at the May Assembly of 1939, the Baptist Union, in accepting the report of the Council, endorsed the Council's own resolution that the Baptist Union should join the proposed World Council. The *Baptist Times* report of 4 May 1939 records that, in introducing the Council's report, Aubrey made an impassioned appeal 'for Unity in these difficult days' and pleaded for a united front 'to show the world what Christianity really means'. The outbreak of the Second World War five months later meant that nine years were to pass before that resolution could be acted upon.

Like Shakespeare before him, Aubrey was involved deeply in Free Church activities. In 1925 there were two Free Church groupings. The older of the two, the Free Church Council was founded in 1895. Its purpose is best summed up by its first President, Dr Charles Berry, at its first Congress:

> This first Congress was born not made ..... This is not a Nonconformist Congress whose *raison d'être* lies in a negative and critical attitude towards the Established Church. This is a Free Church Congress based upon our common and positive adhesion to the great verities of Evangelical history.

In short, it was a united evangelical enterprise by the Free Churches. During the first three decades of this century many evangelical campaigns arose from it, led by Gipsy Smith, Tom Sykes, F.W. Norwood and Lionel Fletcher.

The younger grouping was the Federal Council of Evangelical Free Churches, which grew out of pressures for closer formal relations between the Free Churches. The greatest pleader for its institution and subsequent champion of its cause was none other than J.H. Shakespeare. Speaking as President of the Free Church Council at Bradford in 1918, he brought all his oratorical powers to bear on the issue of Free Church Union.

> To-day I rear upon the battlefield the standard of the United Free Church of England. Let all ready to do battle for the cause gather

beneath its folds.

Not all the Free Churches rallied to this cause. Many Baptists were suspicious, some were strongly opposed, especially because of Shakespeare's evident willingness to consider episcopacy positively. The Methodists, too, were divided. But Shakespeare and others were determined. So the Federal Council of Evangelical Free Churches met for the first time in October 1919.

For the next twenty years the national Free Church Council and the Federal Council of Evangelical Free Churches ran parallel. The two bodies co-operated, however, in a joint committee to consider a joint response by the Free Churches to the 1920 Lambeth Conference's 'Appeal to All Christian People'. Mainly, however, between the two wars they maintained a separate existence with particular emphases, the one on evangelism, the other on the development of relationships between the Free Churches themselves and with the Established Church. Gradually, however, proposals emerged, supported by Aubrey, to unite the two bodies.

Aubrey became Moderator of the Federal Council in 1936 and inherited the accepted responsibility of that office to represent the Free Churches on national occasions. His predecessor, Sidney Berry, had read the lesson at St Paul's in May 1935, at the celebration service for the Silver Jubilee of King George V, and shared in the BBC's memorial service to the King in January 1936.

The Federal Council wrote to the Coronation Claims Committee, suggesting that the Free Churches should play a part in the Coronation Service of Edward VIII, and that the Moderator of the Federal Council, i.e. Aubrey, should be involved. The Archbishop of Canterbury, Cosmo Gordon Lang, responded in November 1936, arguing that the Coronation Service was a unique occasion with ancient tradition behind it and could not be compared to the Silver Jubilee occasion. It was at this point that the Abdication Crisis arose and the Council decided not to press the matter further. The Free Churches were consulted, however, during the difficult days leading up to 10 December, when Edward abdicated.

When George VI was crowned on 12 May 1937, six Free Church representatives, including Aubrey, were present in Westminster Abbey and were part of the Coronation procession. Aubrey shared, also, with the Archbishop of Canterbury and the Moderator of the Church of Scotland in a broadcast service on the Sunday prior to 12 May. Significantly, at the close of his Moderatorship in 1938, Aubrey was made a Companion of Honour by George VI.

During the late 1930s pressure grew for a union of the two Free Church Councils. To most people outside the Councils themselves the reasons for their separate existence were not clear. The international situation became increasingly bleak with the rise of Mussolini and Hitler. Co-operation between all the Churches was becoming a more and more important agenda item. The Free Churches needed one voice. With the declaration of war on 3 September 1939, speed became the essence of the situation. In July 1940, with the war situation critical, the Moderator of the Federal Council and the President of the Free Church Council issued a *Call to Prayer*. On 10 September 1940, in the Council Chamber of the Baptist Church House in Southampton Row in the midst of an air raid, union was achieved and the Free Church Federal Council came into being - a title it retained for very nearly sixty years. In that same Council Chamber in 1942 a wider fellowship was established with the formation of the British Council of Churches under the presidency of William Temple, newly appointed Archbishop of Canterbury.

In all his work Aubrey was surrounded by, and on the whole supported by, a smallish group of distinguished lay people. Both Shakespeare and Aubrey served the Union as Secretary for twenty-six years. During Shakespeare's time there were six Presidents of the Union who were lay. During Aubrey's years there were ten. In the second half of the twentieth century there have been eight. Of Shakespeare's lay Presidents two, Herbert Marnham and T.R. Glover (whose 1924 Presidency coincided with Shakespeare's resignation) continued active into Aubrey's time. These two, together with some of Aubrey's lay Presidents, notably Thomas Penny, Alfred Ellis, H.L. Taylor, Henry Wood, Wilson Black, Seymour Price, Ernest Brown and C.T. Le Quesne, played significant roles in denominational life. They were deeply committed to the life of the Baptist churches together and brought many gifts and important (though sometimes divisive) views to the life of the Union.

Politically, Aubrey's time in office saw a definite weakening of the heretofore assumed firm adherence of Baptists to the Liberal Party. Shakespeare was a firm Liberal and, together with his brother Alfred, saw to it that the newly founded *Baptist Times and Freeman* was supportive of that Party. Lloyd George, so David Bebbington records, had taken pains to court J.H. Shakespeare, whose assistance he invited in dealing with the problems of the nation just before the 1918 General Election.[6] In the 1922 Election, the *Baptist Times* was the only denominational paper to support Lloyd George

---

[6] David Bebbington, 'Baptists and Politics since 1914', in K.W. Clements, *Baptists in the Twentieth Century*, Baptist Historical Society 1982.

wholeheartedly. But by 1924, when J.C. Carlile was acting as Secretary for the year after Shakespeare's resignation, the paper indicated its support for a Conservative government, albeit one which relied upon Liberal support for a majority. The following year Carlile, having handed over the Secretaryship to Aubrey, became editor of the paper. From then on, while implying a Liberal preference, the paper ceased to endorse regularly any particular party at an election.

During the inter-war years there was a retreat from politics by Baptists corporately. This loss of political voice was due, at least in part, to the growing lack of trust in politicians to deliver their promises, not least to the Free Churches.[7] One politician, in particular, Lloyd George, had not 'delivered' in the years following the 1906 election, in which the Baptists, together with many of the other Free Churches, supported him. His personal behaviour and attitudes had disappointed, but it must also be said that the diverse political views amongst leading lay folk of the denomination encouraged circumspection. Baptists together were losing their political will and way - and, truth to tell, never seem to have recovered them since, for never again would there be a focus of support for one party as there had been in the heyday of the Liberal-Nonconformist alliance. Nonconformists were increasingly diverse in their levels of wealth and in their political outlook and were accordingly to be found in all three parties, which effectively led to an exclusion of party politics from denominational discussion.

Aubrey's own politics were by no means clear. The one political issue upon which he made a public and determined stand was that of Lloyd George's 1935 *Call to Action*. A detailed account of this political intervention by the ageing ex-prime minister has been considered extensively by others and Aubrey's vehement opposition to the *Call* has been considered by the present writer elsewhere.[8] Suffice it to record here that the *Call to Action* seems to have been an attempted 'last rally' by the seventy-year-old Lloyd George. The *Call* was issued in March 1935 at the National Council of the Evangelical Free Churches. It drew attention to the need for speedy action on unemployment and in foreign affairs, notably relationships with Germany and how to 'keep the peace'. This launch was followed on 5 June by a press statement from Lloyd George, that at the instigation of a number of well-known Nonconformists, he was planning a nationwide campaign to rouse public

---

[7] See Michael Goodman, op.cit.
[8] W.M.S. West, 'The Reverend Secretary Aubrey - Part I', *Baptist Quarterly* XXXIV.5, 1992, pp.204ff.

opinion on the issues of peace and unemployment. A manifesto was drawn up which church leaders were invited to sign.

There was turmoil amongst Free Church leaders, particularly the Baptists. Some were enthusiastic, others dubious and a few hostile. Aubrey fell initially between the latter two groups, but quickly grew hostile to the proposals. His public utterances indicated that he thought the manifesto quite unfair to the efforts of the current government. S.W. Hughes, R. Wilson Black, both officers of the Evangelical Free Church Council, and F.W. Norwood, all of them Baptist leaders, were enthusiastic. Aubrey telegraphed them all to say that in his judgement they were seriously mistaken in their support. But when the manifesto was published their names appeared, together with those of Charles Brown and J.C. Carlile, two more leading Baptists. Whereupon Aubrey resigned from the Evangelical Free Church Council.

Eventually and quite quickly the whole episode fizzled out. Lloyd George felt let down by the Free Church leaders. A.J.P. Taylor commented on the episode that Lloyd George 'tried to move the Nonconformist Conscience, his original love. This existed no longer or could not be rallied as a political force'. It would be truer to say that in so far as it existed it could not be rallied as a political force. This was seventy-five years ago. It is questionable whether anything has changed.

Aubrey's vehement attitude to this issue is explained, in part, by his own words written to William Olney, a Baptist layman in London: 'I have myself made perfectly clear to the Prime Minister and others when they have consulted me, that as the leader of the Baptist Union, I could never play any party game.'[9] This was not simply because of the diversity of political viewpoint amongst leading lay figures, nor to the elevation to Cabinet rank early in June of another Baptist lay leader, Ernest Brown, who became Minister of Labour, but to Aubrey's personal conviction that party politics belonged to the sphere of independent individual Christian decision, not upon interdependent Christian statement and action. Such a view accords well with the strong strain of pragmatism which characterized Aubrey's make up.

Nevertheless, it is worthy of note that during Shakespeare's and Aubrey's secretaryships there is clear evidence to suggest that they were from time to time in their *ex officio* capacity consulted by Prime Ministers. How many, one wonders, of the four subsequent secretaries of the Union were similarly consulted pro-actively by Prime Ministers?

---

[9] W.M.S. West, 'The Reverend Secretary Aubrey - Part I', *Baptist Quarterly* XXXIV.5, 1992, p.212.

When Baldwin called an election later that year, on 14 November 1935, 432 candidates supporting the National Government were returned, as against 154 Labour members and only twenty Liberals, four of whom were members of Lloyd George's family. Yet the victory in that election hinted at another, new scenario developing, for the voting figures showed 11.8 million votes for the government and 8.3 million votes for Labour. If personal experience and recollection have any evidential value, amongst the 8.3 million there were a growing number of 'rank and file' Baptists. The growing tide of Labour support was to swamp both the Conservatives and the Liberals when the next election was held a decade later in the last months of the Second World War. The distribution of the Free Church vote across the three parties made it increasingly difficult for the Union and the local church to address the political agenda with vigour and precision.

During Aubrey's time in office the Department structure of the Baptist Union developed apace. In 1927 the appointment of Dr T.G. Dunning to the responsibilities of Temperance, Social Service and Youth showed widening concerns. The leadership of the Women's Department passed to Miss Doris Rose and the significance of women's contribution to the life of the denomination increased notably. Although a few women had served as Baptist ministers for more than a decade, in 1934 the Baptist Union Council formally agreed and acknowledged their eligibility for admission to the ministry.

The Council itself increased in numbers and in the liveliness of its debates. During the mid-1930s a group of younger Council members formed a group entitled 'Focus', which met on the evening prior to the Council to talk over denominational affairs in general and major topics on the Council's agenda in particular. To read the names of the members of Focus is fascinating in that many of them later became significant members of the 'Establishment' of the Union, where they in turn would act in the role of 'poacher turned gamekeeper'! They included J.O. Barrett, Frank Bryan, Robert Child, Charles Jewson, Ingli James, J.B. Middlebrook and Ernest Payne. It is evident they were critical of the official line and they did not hesitate to say so. To the officers of the day, whatever the group might call itself, its criticisms appeared to be those of a pressure group without clearly 'focused' alternative policies. Union life, in common with all history, has a habit of repeating itself and something similar, but much more clearly 'focused' and organized, was to happen again some forty years later.

From time to time during the Aubrey years evident theological tensions manifested themselves. They were not new: most of them dated at least from the final decades of the nineteenth century. One was the question of attitudes to biblical criticism and the authority and 'inspiration' of the Scriptures, notably the Authorized Version. Another had to do with understandings of the Kingdom of God: was it an event which would be fulfilled by a divine cataclysmic action or was it a process that could be progressed by human endeavour with divine assistance - or might it be something of both? Then there was the debate on Science and Religion, seen then by some in terms of God in Genesis chapter one versus Evolution. Not entirely disassociated from these was the issue of the doctrine of Atonement. Was it to be explained fundamentally (and for some solely) on the basis of a substitutionary theory of Christ's death on the cross or were other doctrines also permissible? In particular, still in the 1930s, and in a way related to all these issues, lay the actual memory (for a few) and the inherited tradition (for a much larger number) of the Down Grade Controversy of the late 1880s which had resulted in C.H. Spurgeon's resignation from the Union.

One particular illustration of the underlying tensions surfacing within the Union came in 1932. This was the publication of a group study outline written by T.R. Glover for the Baptist Union and entitled *Fundamentals*. This publication was intended to help initiate a Discipleship Campaign. Within it Glover had questioned the uniqueness of the substitutionary theory of the Atonement. The cry of 'Modernist' was raised against Glover and, because it was a Union publication, implicitly against the Union itself. In the event, moderation on both sides prevented very serious repercussions. Aubrey, in a letter written some twenty-five years after these events, speaks of how the aftermath of the Down Grade Controversy was still evident in the Union's life during his secretaryship. While not necessarily always related to that Controversy, the theological tensions which it represented have reappeared from time to time to challenge the Union's 'Baptist togetherness' throughout the twentieth century.

The inter-war years showed a continuing population move from the inner cities with a speedy development of 'suburbia'. During Aubrey's later years as Secretary these moves from the town centres were hastened by local Council developments on the outskirts to aid what was known as 'slum clearance'. Many suburbs were developed through voluntary movement, helped by the speedy increase in house purchase and more building societies with mortgages available, but municipal developments were more a directly interventional process of 'uprooting' families. They were moved from the familiar to the unfamiliar not only in neighbourhood terms but also the type of housing. Former rural areas were embraced within the new suburbia but not all existing churches caught up in such social changes were able to rise to the new missionary opportunities on their doorsteps, underlining the need for the development of a strategy of 'Baptists Together' to face new challenges.

As Shakespeare in his day was concerned to develop Baptist church life in the cities of late Victorian England, so now Aubrey and his colleagues were eager to meet the evangelistic challenge of this population movement outwards. From 1935-38 the Union had a full-time Evangelist and Commissioner for Evangelism. In 1936 the Baptist Forward Movement was launched. This had as its twin aims evangelism in the 'new' areas of population and the raising of money to support new buildings. In 1949 Aubrey initiated the 'Baptist Advance' project and devoted much of his time to it over the final two years of his secretaryship, including his last year in office, 1950-51, when he was also the President of the Union. Under Aubrey a new Home Work Fund Scheme, set up in 1947, included provision for the special financial support of initial pastorates in new causes, largely in the new areas of population. By greater efficiency through co-ordinated special appeals and a consequent re-organization of the Union's finances, this Home Work Scheme opened up new possibilities for the stipends of aided ministers.   As a result, the sense of interdependence within the Union was considerably enhanced, with constant emphasis on the financing of churches through the Fund being one of mutual denominational aid, with the larger and more prosperous churches sharing financially and in other ways with those in less affluent circumstances. Such sense of mutuality amongst Baptists has always lain, ideally, at the root of Baptist togetherness. In the post-war days, in the aftermath of years of shared suffering and then shared victory, that sense surfaced rather more naturally and willingly than in more recent years with a growingly acquisitive society. Mutuality is now rather more 'against the tide' than it was in 1947: this makes currently maintained giving to the present Home Mission Fund all the more encouraging.

Throughout Shakespeare's time and on into Aubrey's, the relationships between the Union and the Baptist Missionary Society were good. In 1936 B. Grey Griffith was BMS Home Secretary and much involved in Union affairs. That year the possibility arose that the nearby Patent Office, which needed to expand its Furnival Street premises, might well seek to purchase the BMS building. The leadership of the BMS raised the issue with the Union as to whether this might provide an opportunity to seek a new denominational headquarters to be shared with the Union. The suggestion was welcomed by the Union, but with caution. The Southampton Row premises were only thirty years old, were well situated and more than adequate for the Union's work.

But by November 1936 the Union's Council was willing to pass an enabling resolution stating the principle 'that the members of the Council of the Baptist Union consider it desirable that the work of the Baptist Missionary Society and of the Baptist Union should, if possible, be carried on in the same building'. It is probable some Union Council members had in mind the possibility of the BMS moving into Southampton Row. The BMS showed little enthusiasm for this suggestion and it became soon evident that this was not viable for a number of practical reasons also, including insufficient space.

With this possibility ruled out, evident reluctance - and indeed opposition - surfaced on the Union's side, but negotiations continued. A joint sub-committee from Union and Society was set up. It might be thought that, as H.L. Taylor of Bristol, the BMS Treasurer, was the Union's President for 1937-8, the path might be smooth. In fact, it turned out to be very rough. One of the chief supporters on the Union side was R. Wilson Black of the Twynholm Church which, until it joined the Baptist Union in 1931, had been an influential member of the Churches of Christ. Wilson Black was a layman of energy, foresight and generosity. He was a supporter in advocacy and finance of both the Union's Evangelist, J.N. Britten, and of the Forward Movement. He was also well-versed in the property market in London. He discovered a site in Russell Square which would provide 75,000 square feet of office space and was available on a leasehold of 200 years. Some Union leaders, however, objected to the purchase of a leasehold site and certainly one which would require the Union and Society to let more than half of it commercially as the two Baptist groups required only 35,000 square feet between them.

There were serious divisions within the Union on the issue and also division, though less serious, from the Society's side.[10] A number of the BMS representatives on the joint committee were, of course, members also of the Union's Council. In any case, any scheme would have to go to the Assembly. In March 1938 the Union's Council, by a majority vote of 64 to 28, agreed that the scheme for the Russell Square site could go to the Assembly as a Council recommendation. Yet H.L. Taylor and A.S. Clark, Treasurers of the BMS and Union respectively, were both against. Not surprisingly, notice of a wrecking amendment blocking the scheme appeared on the order paper for the Assembly. In spite of Wilson Black's best efforts the amendment was carried and was subsequently accepted as the substantive motion.

---

[10] Elsewhere I have told in detail the story of the protracted negotiations which followed: W.M.S. West, 'The Reverend Secretary Aubrey - Part II', *Baptist Quarterly* XXXIV.6, 1992, pp.263ff.

The aftermath was difficult for Aubrey. Wilson Black decided to resign from Council, convinced that he had been let down by the Union and its officers, particularly by Aubrey. But prolonged negotiations and commonsense overcame the problem. Wilson Black was persuaded not to resign; the Baptist Forward movement he championed still went forward; the BMS remained in Furnival Street until war came, when they were evacuated to Kettering; Furnival Street was destroyed in the blitz; Southampton Row survived, though not without damage; but it took another fifty years before what was seemingly the general desire of the Baptist denomination throughout the whole period was achieved and Society and Union moved in under one roof in a planned, harmonized diversity.

Throughout the Aubrey years, the denomination had to live with declining membership. In 1926 the membership was 416,000; by 1946 it was 355,000 and this against a rising total population. The loss in Sunday School scholars was even more striking: from 525,000 in 1926 to 302,000 in 1946. These were the days of my own childhood, adolescence and early manhood. Retrospectively, one can perceive now how the leisure life of the local community at large detached itself from the life of the local church communities. There was now so much else to do, more attractive and less demanding than the church-organized leisure activities.

The Union's reaction to this, in addition to the attempts at special evangelical efforts, was corporately to resort to *ad hoc* commissions of enquiry. In 1936 a Commission on Baptist Polity was set up. This eventually presented its final report in November 1942. As its title suggests, this had more to do with how the denomination organized its life than with declining membership. Its final report sought to strengthen the churches by strengthening and encouraging the ministry. There is clearly wisdom in this for, as Richard Baxter said, 'All the Churches either rise or fall as the ministry doth rise and fall - not in riches and worldly grandeur - but in knowledge, zeal and ability for their work'. This report was one of the earliest in a line of reports on the ministry which have flowed from the Union in the past sixty years.

In 1944 the Council discussed the 'State of the Churches' in what Ernest Payne called an 'anxious debate'. As a result a special group was set up, convened by the Revd Henry Cook, to look at the situation more closely. In 1946 the Union published the group's report with the title, *Speak that they go forward*. It challenged the churches to rethink the Christian message and called them to more aggressive evangelism. A number of 'campaigns' of evangelism were led by Henry Cook and others, largely spearheaded by the Board of General Superintendents on which Henry Cook represented the Metropolitan Area. There were many ministerial candidates and the colleges were full.[11] Student life within the universities was vibrant and religious societies flourished, both denominational and those more broadly based. The Baptist Students Federation was founded to stimulate Baptist community and loyalty. There were youth rallies at Assemblies and the Young People's Departments of both the Baptist Missionary Society and the Union were proactive. The BMS Summer Schools in particular were popular and effective, notably with younger people, and initiated many a Baptist romance.

Politically the country saw a new beginning with the decisive victory of the Labour Party at the 1945 Election and its determination to realize in practice the welfare state. Aubrey himself was active in 'buying up' the seemingly new opportunities on offer. His own reputation had been enhanced by his appointment in 1947 to the Royal Commission on the Press. Now, as he prepared to retire, he determined to return to his 'evangelistic pastoral mode'. The Baptist Advance campaign was initiated in this context.

The world had 'shrunk' during the war and horizons had widened. Aubrey and others saw the importance of renewing and developing wider contacts. He continued his ecumenical activities with the Faith and Order and Life and Work movements and was a delegate to the First World Council of Churches Assembly at Amsterdam in 1948. He encouraged support for the Baptist World Alliance and for the urgent development of contacts with European Baptists who needed support in recovery and literal rebuilding.

When he retired in 1951, Aubrey had served the Union as Secretary for twenty-six years, the same time as Shakespeare. No other Secretary since has served so long. He had consolidated and developed the life of Baptists together. The Union had a higher profile amongst the churches in 1951 than it had had in 1926. He had held together the diverse viewpoints within the denomination in a broad consensus - sometimes too broad for some to accept easily. In retirement he could look back with satisfaction on the consolidation and expansion of the work of the Union during a period of unusual difficulty. The denomination was more aware of itself, its opportunities, its strengths and its weaknesses.

---

[11] This report came out during my first year as a student in Bristol Baptist College. We were a group of relatively old students 'back from the war'. There was a spirit of hopefulness abroad. Indeed, it was a spirit of optimism. Scarcely a long vacation went by without the conduct of an evangelistic campaign, or more than one.

3 - E.A. PAYNE

On Thursday, 26 April 1951, at the morning session of the Baptist Union Assembly held at Bloomsbury a new General Secretary of the Baptist Union to succeed M.E. Aubrey was welcomed. His name was Ernest Alexander Payne. Almost exactly twenty-five years earlier, as a student at Regent's Park College, he had sat in the Bloomsbury gallery and witnessed the welcome of M.E. Aubrey to the Secretaryship. He had wondered then whether the fluent welcome and high-sounding commitment of the Assembly to Aubrey would be maintained in constant support over the subsequent years.

As Ernest Payne stood in the Bloomsbury pulpit on that April Thursday in 1951 he knew only too well that the Aubrey years had not been without their hard times when loyalties had been tested and earlier affirmations of support had, in the realities of denominational life, not always been maintained. Such thoughts must have been in Ernest Payne's mind as he heard the President of the Union, Dr H.R. Williamson, quote these words concerning his appointment from the Council's Report for 1950:

> On those who have chosen him lies the moral and inescapable obligation of supporting him with their prayers and loyalty in his heavy task of leadership. The Council looks to the future with high hopes and assures Mr Payne of its willing co-operation and affectionate solicitude for him and Mrs Payne in their new sphere.

One wonders who penned those words in the Report. It could well have been M.E. Aubrey reminding Council and the wider denomination of its responsibility towards the Secretary not for a day, not for a year, but for the whole term of office.

Be that as it may, Ernest Payne replied in his typically succinct style. After indicating his apprehension about the task, he went on to say, 'I accept from you this solemn trust and responsibility. Relying on the pledge of this company here, and those whom they represent, and relying upon God, I will serve the denomination'.

So began another significant chapter in the story of 'Baptists together' in the twentieth century.

* * * * * * * * *

Ernest Payne was born on 19 February 1902, the eldest of three children of Alexander Payne, partner in an accountancy firm bearing his name, and Catherine, daughter of Philip Griffiths, a Baptist minister who trained at Stepney College and served for many years at Biggleswade in Bedfordshire. The whole family became deeply involved in the life of the Downs Baptist Church in Clapton. Ernest Payne, from his earliest years in Hackney Downs Secondary School, showed academic promise. In October 1919 he entered King's College London to study for a general arts degree, followed by an Honours Degree in Philosophy.

His desire was to serve the Baptist Missionary Society overseas. With this in mind, in October 1922 he entered Regent's Park College, then in London, gaining the degree of Bachelor of Divinity from London University.

At Regent's Park College he came under the influence of the Principal, Henry Wheeler Robinson. His was a personality to which the word 'extraordinary' aptly applied. Some found him austere; certainly he was very demanding upon himself, his family and his students. He was ahead of almost everybody in facing every intellectual issue and, indeed, it seemed to his students, in reading every book! In leading worship, in particular at the College weekly communion services (a frequency of celebration rare amongst Baptists seventy-five years ago), he generated a spiritual force so strong that it overflowed into the lives of those around him, kindling and enriching them. Perhaps it is not surprising that one of his most significant books is entitled *The Christian Experience of the Holy Spirit*.

In College days too Payne was impressed by A.E. Garvie, the Principal of New College, the Congregational college in London, with which Regent's co-operated in shared lecturing. Garvie was a pioneer in the inter-church relationships then developing both nationally in responding to the 1920 Lambeth Appeal and internationally in the development of Life and Work and of Faith and Order. He was also Chairman of the 1924 Birmingham conference on Politics, Economics and Citizenship (COPEC) about which students then in the theological college had a number of study groups.

The effect of these two Principals on Ernest Payne was to inculcate in him a deep loyalty and life-long commitment to Regent's Park College and to plant in him both an unshakeable conviction of the Christian imperative for church relating beyond his own beloved Baptist denomination, and also an essential concern for relationship between church and society.

Payne's college years were clouded by the health problems of his younger brother and sister. This raised questions as to the wisdom of his serving overseas with the Baptist Missionary Society. As an interim measure in October 1925 he took up a place offered to him at Mansfield College, Oxford. Here he studied Sanskrit and wrote a thesis on the Saka movement in Hinduism, obtaining in 1927 the degree of Bachelor of Letters.

During his student days at Mansfield, Payne was involved on Wheeler Robinson's behalf in searching for a possible site which could enable Regent's Park College to move to Oxford. One afternoon in June 1926 Payne was sent to call on a Mr J.T. Dodd, the owner of 55 St Giles and some nearby property. Mr Dodd had lived all his life in 55 St Giles, as had his father before him, but now he had decided to move to the South Coast and, although an Anglican, was sympathetic to the possibility of the property being bought and developed by good Protestant Baptists! So that June afternoon Payne stood on the spot now occupied by the Helwys Hall but then the site of old stables. He saw immediately the potential of the property for Regent's. He went back to Mansfield and wrote an excited letter to Wheeler Robinson commending the possibilities of the site for a new college. By 1927 negotiations were complete and later that year Payne helped to unpack Wheeler Robinson's books when he moved into 55 St Giles.

After a final semester spent in Marburg University which lasted until March 1928, Payne decided to seek ministerial settlement in England. On 23 October 1928 he was ordained and inducted to the pastorate of Bugbrooke Baptist Church in Northamptonshire. In 1932 he accepted an invitation to become Young People's Secretary of the Baptist Missionary Society where he became acquainted with the Revd B. Grey Griffith, then BMS Home Secretary. Their developing friendship was to be of some significance for the story of Baptists together. In 1936 Payne was appointed editorial secretary of the Society and began to develop his considerable talent for writing. His office meant that he attended committees of the United Council for Missionary Education at Edinburgh House, bringing him into contact with younger members of the various other denominational headquarters' staff, who later would develop into his companions in the ecumenical movement. In the Edinburgh House context too he had had contact with first-generation ecumenical leaders such as William Paton and J.H. Oldham.

In 1935, on the sudden death of C.M. Hardy, Payne became secretary to the Regent's Park College Council. He was a member also of the House and Finance Committee and his involvement in the College deepened, as did his contacts with leading Baptist laymen - all successful in their respective professions: Cecil Rooke, the Baptist Union Solicitor, H.H. Collier, an estate agent, C.T. Le Quesne, a barrister, Seymour Price, an insurance broker,

Herbert Chown. a stockbroker, and Herbert Marnham, Treasurer of the Baptist Union.

Whilst at the BMS, in 1934, Payne was invited by J.H. Rushbrooke to address the Fifth Baptist World Congress in Berlin on the subject of 'Anti-God propaganda', with special reference to the situation in Russia. Grey Griffith encouraged Payne to accept. The Berlin experience was significant for Payne as a person and for his reputation.

1934 saw the rise of Hitler, who had become Chancellor the previous year. During the BWA Congress Hindenburg, the elder statesman and President of Germany, died. His death ended a chapter in post-1918 German history; many Germans, especially discerning German Christians, realized that the next chapter would hold many changes and uncertainties for them. During the Congress itself, the wife of a leading German Baptist minister, a woman of Czech origin whose husband Payne had known during his Marburg semester in 1928, took Payne aside, led him to a secluded place behind the platform and spoke to him with concern and apprehension about the dangers now facing Christians - and indeed the whole German people. Others too spoke with Payne in Berlin of their fear of the future. He was learning fast the complexities of international Christian relationships.

Payne's paper attracted a good deal of attention. J.H. Oldham, who was already preparing material for the proposed 1937 Oxford Conference on Church, Community and State in connection with the Life and Work movement, heard about Payne from Rushbrooke and immediately sent him drafts of preliminary pamphlets for his comments and an invitation to meet. This stimulated still further Payne's own interest in the developing ecumenical movement.

Not surprisingly, he was invited to participate in the Sixth Congress of the Baptist World Alliance in Atlanta, Georgia, in July 1939. Not only did he write 'A Pageant of Baptist History' (subsequently published in 1942 under the title of *Missionaries All*), but he was invited to speak on 'Youth and Baptist Values'. He was thirty-seven at the time. His address was brief and to the point. It shows his ability to summarize arguments. What he defined then as the five points of the Baptist Faith which he argued were perpetually relevant are perhaps all too easily assumed and even taken for granted today. They were:

1) the necessity of individual faith and conviction
2) the practice of believer's baptism
3) the church as a spiritual fellowship made up of converted men and

women
4) the missionary impetus and personal evangelism
5) a passion for liberty.

He drew attention to the relative youth of some Baptist pioneers. Thomas Helwys was not much more than thirty years old when he founded the first Baptist Church in England and Roger Williams about thirty when he established Rhode Island Colony. William Carey was thirty-four when he reached India. Tom Comber was twenty-four when he went to Africa. C.H. Spurgeon's preaching ministry began in his 'teens and his London ministry commenced in his twenties.

Developments in Regent's Park College occupied much of Payne's spare time. The foundation stone of the new college buildings in Oxford were laid on 21 July 1938 and he was much involved with Wheeler Robinson in fund-raising. There were decisions to be taken as to whether to continue with the building work as the outbreak of war became inevitable and how to pay for it. It was decided to proceed: the sixteen study bedrooms were completed in the summer of 1940, just before the government clamped down on private building.

It was not surprising to others, therefore, when in 1940 Payne was asked to join the staff at Oxford. But the invitation apparently astonished Payne himself. His immediate reaction to the invitation was negative. He believed that his life's work would be for the Missionary Society - if not abroad, then at home. He had not kept up his theological reading to any serious degree. The BMS did not want to lose him. But a few influential friends thought otherwise. H.R. Williamson, since 1938 the Foreign Secretary of the Society, doubted whether Payne's many gifts could ever be fully utilized by the BMS. Grey Griffith, while making quite clear that the decision must be Payne's, reminded him that he must now consider not only the present but also his future. He was thirty-eight and what today would be called his 'career development' should not be overlooked. In addition, Wheeler Robinson needed him. Wheeler was now sixty-eight years old and had been carrying much of the burden of the move to Oxford, the development of the site, and the ongoing work of the college almost single-handed.

So in June 1940, albeit initially somewhat reluctantly, Payne moved to Oxford, where he was to stay for eleven years. At college he taught Christian doctrine, comparative religion and church history, becoming an acknowledged expert on the Anabaptists. For six years he was University lecturer in comparative religion and history of modern mission. He was a popular tutor, enjoying the stimulus of teaching and discussion. He produced three significant books: *The Church Awakes* (1942), which is an outline history of the modern missionary movement, *The Free Church Tradition in the Life of England* (1944), and *The Fellowship of Believers: Baptist thought and practice yesterday and today* (1952).

During the late 1930s his impact in Baptist Union affairs developed. Probably because of the attention drawn to him by his 1934 Berlin address, he was co-opted on to the Baptist Union Council. As mentioned earlier, he became a member of a group of younger Council members known as 'Focus', whose members met prior to Council meetings to discuss major topics on the agenda and their reactions to them. In this context he renewed contact with J.O. Barrett, a former student at Rawdon with whom in college days he had sought to link together more closely the students of the various Baptist colleges. At the end of 1926 they had organized a conference at the Baptist Church House where every college was represented. The students discovered that there existed among them a real desire to start something more permanent so there came into existence the Baptist Theological Students Union, which continued, with fluctuating fortunes, until just after the Second World War when it was one of the contributing streams which led to the formation of the Baptist Students Federation. Not surprisingly, Payne during his Secretarial years was a great encourager and supporter of this Federation.

Whilst Payne may have been unaware of it, others were recognizing him as a potential leader amongst Baptists. It is rather more likely that Payne did not want to dwell too much on such a possibility. He was well content in Oxford, he loved the College, he enjoyed his work, he wanted time to write. He had so much he would like to do. He cherished the hope (never fulfilled) that he would be able to produce a definitive history of the Baptist Missionary Society.

But others saw his wider potential as his involvements proliferated. As early as 1944 an attempt was made to nominate him for the vice-presidency of the Baptist Union. To say he was reluctant to stand is an overstatement! When he discovered that Dr Dakin, the Principal of Bristol Baptist College, was a definite candidate, Payne found what he judged to be a cast-iron case for not standing, lest it be thought that it could be a case of inter-college rivalry - or, worse still, of personal rivalry. For he disagreed strongly with certain views expressed by Dakin in his soon to be published *The Baptist View of the Church and Ministry*.

When the war ended and foreign travel became again possible, Payne resumed his activities with the Baptist World Alliance. He attended the 1947

Copenhagen Congress. J.H. Rushbrooke had died in 1946 and there was a considerable shift of leadership of the Alliance from Europe, particularly Britain, to the United States. Copenhagen took the decision to establish a headquarters in Washington DC. That Congress also debated Baptist membership of the proposed World Council of Churches. Some delegates, especially those from the American Southern Baptist Convention, were critical of the proposal and of possible Baptist membership. An attempt was made to remit decision about any Baptist membership to the Executive Committee of the Alliance, where Americans had the dominant voice. Payne intervened in the debate and pointed out two vital constitutional issues. The first was that the proposed World Council of Churches was to be a council of *churches* with which world confessional organizations such as the BWA would have only a *fraternal* relationship. The second was that the BWA's constitution itself made it clear that the Alliance could not interfere with the policies and decisions of individual Unions and Conventions. He submitted on a point of order that on these two counts the motion proposed was invalid. This challenge was accepted by the chairman and the proposal was dropped. In spite of this (or possibly because of it!) Payne found himself elected to the Executive of the Alliance.

There is a paradox at the heart of Payne's personality. On the one hand his personal convictions were so deep that he felt bound to express his views on major issues, always clearly, cogently and concisely argued, yet on the other hand he seemed to have little desire to accept that others saw in him a person of great personal gifts and leadership potential. There is extant a remarkable fifty-years correspondence between his great friend, J.O. Barrett, and himself. More than once Barrett reproaches Payne for his apparent lack of ambition. Barrett feared that such a lack could prevent Payne from using to the full the great gifts with which he had been endowed.

This issue was to be put to test yet again in 1949 when W.O. Lewis, Associate Secretary of the BWA, came to see Payne in Oxford with the news that he was expecting to retire the following year and hoped Payne would accept nomination as his successor. This approach was supported by Theodore Adams, one of the most influential of the Americans in the BWA. Lewis hinted that, if appointed, such a post would almost certainly lead him to be appointed General Secretary of the Alliance in a year or two's time. Payne flatly refused the nomination.

Yet again in 1951 another question arose, this time in connection with a possible return to the BMS. The Foreign Secretary, H.R. Williamson, was to retire in 1951. Payne was appointed Chairman of the Secretariat Committee which was considering various ways forward into the future, both of structure and of personnel. Payne was suddenly confronted by a suggestion from within the committee that he should accept nomination to succeed Williamson. Devoted as he was to the BMS, he did not feel that this was the way forward for him or for the BMS. He had had virtually no firsthand experience of missionary work overseas and his relationship with J.B. Middlebrook, the BMS Home Secretary, had for a number of years been somewhat uneasy.

But he was not to be left in peace in his beloved Regent's. By 1950 M.E. Aubrey would have reached the age of sixty-five. There was a general desire that for his final year of office as Secretary he should also be President of the Union. He was therefore elected Vice-President in 1949 and so would enter the Presidency in the spring of 1950. A committee under the chairmanship of Percy Evans was set up to recommend through Council to the Assembly the name of a successor. Clear evidence suggests that Payne had no real expectation and certainly no particular desire that the committee would look in his direction.

Percy Evans, who retired as Principal of Spurgeon's College in 1950, had come to know Payne well as a Baptist colleague in the conversations between sixteen Anglicans and sixteen Free Church representatives following Archbishop Fisher's Cambridge sermon of 3 November 1946, which suggested that consideration should be given by the Free Churches to taking 'episcopacy into their systems'. Of the three Baptists appointed, Evans, Payne and J. Ingli-James, Payne was the most knowledgeable on ecumenical affairs and within the Oxford context already knew a number of the Anglican participants. Evans, the leader of the Baptist group, relied considerably upon Payne, whom he used sometimes to call his 'armour bearer'. Evans recognized Payne's intellectual and negotiating skills and the value of his wider ecumenical contacts. At one point Leonard Hodgson, an Anglican and Regius Professor of Theology at Oxford, and Ernest Payne were asked to prepare complementary papers on episcopacy. Payne's was an incisive piece of writing based on firm biblical and theological principles clearly illustrated from history. These conversations were drawing towards their close when Evans's Committee began to meet to decide Aubrey's successor. By then Payne had begun his wider contacts with Faith and Order at the world level and, with Percy Evans and others, had attended the First Assembly of the World Council of Churches at Amsterdam in 1948.

Whatever Payne may have thought, the nomination committee quickly came to the conclusion that Ernest Payne was its first and clear choice. So on 16 January 1950 Payne received a letter asking him to meet a deputation from the Secretariat Committee. The meeting took place in the offices of the SCM Press. The deputation numbered three, Percy Evans, Arnold Clark (Treasurer of the Union) and Hugh Martin. They presented Payne with a unanimous and pressing invitation to succeed M.E. Aubrey. Payne's initial reaction was one of genuine and deep dismay. He did not want to leave Oxford. He doubted whether he had the requisite gifts - he was not naturally a public figure, nor was he a particularly effective speaker to large gatherings and certainly could not match the oratorical gifts of Shakespeare and Aubrey. What about Regent's Park College and his own developing plans for research and writing? His contact with and knowledge of certain areas of the denomination, particularly what could then still be called the 'Spurgeonic' tradition, were few indeed. So he asked for time to consider and to consult. He turned to those whose judgements he trusted most: Grey Griffith, C.T. Le Quesne, Seymour Price, his brother Philip Payne, and, of course, Percy Evans. What Evans said carried particular weight with him. Evans assured Payne that he would help him to develop positive relationships with those of the Spurgeon tradition.

Payne agreed reluctantly that his name could go to the Baptist Union Council in March 1950 as the sole nomination. At that Council, F.G. Benskin, who had been the minister at the Downs Chapel during Payne's childhood years, proposed the nomination which was warmly and unanimously supported. So it was that in April 1950 his name came to the Baptist Union Assembly with a view to his appointment as Secretary of the Baptist Union for an initial five-year period from May 1951. The recommendation was accepted unanimously and on 26 April the following year he was formally welcomed into the secretaryship with warm words of greeting and assurances of support.

Those of us who were students at Regent's Park College at the time, and who knew him as well as most, had little doubt as to the rightness of the appointment. But we viewed his departure from Oxford, as he did himself, with considerable sadness. We sought to congratulate him, but he replied: 'You may not congratulate me, but you may wish me well'. That summed up accurately his feelings as he contemplated the future.

As for the Union, Baptists together, they had appointed with apparent enthusiasm a person with a known track record of utter loyalty to the Baptist denomination, born of nurture and conviction, a scholar of merit, a person known to be committed to ecumenicity, and a man naturally somewhat shy and very different in temperament from the more extrovert personalities of his two predecessors. He accepted the call to serve out of loyalty to the denomination and because he had been convinced by others that the call truly reflected the will of God.

It may be said that the next sixteen years did not contradict the rightness of that judgement. Like Shakespeare and Aubrey before him, Payne brought to the office all that he could bring - namely himself - and like his predecessors he used his gifts to the full in the service of Baptists together. But, as had his predecessors, he suffered criticism from time to time simply because he remained true to his convictions, which were known when he was appointed.

It is not my intention in reflecting on Ernest Payne's secretaryship to deal in detail with the extraordinarily diversity and development of his sixteen years of office. I have already sought to perform that task in my memoir of him.[11] My purpose here is to seek to assess his particular contributions to the fascinating development over this century of Baptists together.

The 1950 Report of the Baptist Union Council, presented to the 1951 Assembly, which covered Aubrey's last year and ushered in Payne's years, gives a mixed impression of the inheritance bequeathed to Payne. The Korean War cast a cloud over the international situation, coming so soon after the initial 'clear shining after rain' experienced by many, particularly returning service men, at the end of World War II. There was apprehension of the possible outbreak of World War III. Denominationally the Report reminded its readers of the growth of the Superannuation Fund, the establishment of the Home Work Fund and the carrying through of the Baptist Forward Movement. There were signs of consolidation and reconstruction after the trauma of the previous decade, but churches were facing difficulties financially, the need for increasing ministerial stipends and security, and the changing attitudes towards the church of a growingly secular post-war generation. In general, Payne continued these policies, notably in encouraging the reconstruction of bombed church buildings, and supporting the development of new churches, particularly through special grants for initial pastorates in new areas of building. He sought to enlarge the various finances and laid much emphasis upon the new Home Work Fund Scheme for support of ministers in the smaller churches.

One of Payne's gifts - often insufficiently recognized - was the way in which he was able to create a sense of loyalty and mutual support amongst those who worked with him. This was particularly true in his early days in Baptist Church House when he needed it most. Leonard Shugnell, the Union Accountant, who had been in Church House since the days of J.H.

---

[11] W.M.S. West, *To be a pilgrim: a memoir of Ernest A. Payne*, Guildford 1983.

Shakespeare, was one such. Another was O.D. Wiles, the Deputy General Secretary since 1948, a former army chaplain who had ben decorated for service during both world wars, gaining both the DSO and the MC.

B. Grey Griffith, Payne's former mentor of BMS days, was now extremely active in Baptist Union affairs. He had helped decisively with the organization and launching of the new Home Work Fund Scheme and now chaired the Grants Executive Committee. He had an extraordinary knowledge of churches and ministers and, although in his mid-seventies when Payne took office, maintained an astonishing zest for life. As an ex-President he was an active member of the Baptist Union Council in those days before ageism was a serious factor. Younger members of Council remember with gratitude his vigour, wit, wisdom and encouragement - and also that if they 'crossed swords' with him on any issue they did so at their peril, unless of course they turned out to be right - a very rare event! - when he was magnanimous in defeat. Payne always maintained that Grey Griffith had a kind of radar system by which he knew what was happening in Baptist circles. When on 16 September 1958 Payne suffered a heart attack just as he was entering the Baptist Church House, within an hour Grey Griffith was in the House offering support and encouragement to all the staff who were naturally in a state of shock.

It was Grey Griffith who in 1961 proposed the re-appointment of Payne for another five years. In so doing he gave an apt and concise description of Payne's strength. Griffith described Payne as a man with a sense of what was vital, possessed of courage to proceed when others doubted. He suggested that Payne could see the problems that required solving and, although to see a problem is not to solve it, never to see it is never to solve it. He recalled that Payne never spoke without having something worthwhile to say, never spoke except relevantly to the occasion of speaking, was possessed of hindsight, insight and foresight, and knew which was which and which to use at any given moment.

When in 1961 Grey Griffith died in his eighty-fifth year, Payne acknowledged the debt the denomination owed to him by writing a brief memoir, aptly entitled 'Veteran Warrior', which is a quotation from William Cowper, written about an unnamed Christian (probably John Wesley). Cowper's words fittingly describe the Grey Griffith remembered so vividly by those who knew him!

> Yet above all, his luxury supreme,
> And his chief glory, was the gospel theme;

> There he was copious as old Greece or Rome,
> His happy eloquence seemed there at home,
> Ambitious not to strive or to excel,
> But to treat justly what he loved so well.

There were indeed 'giants in the land' in those days - or so it seemed to those of a younger generation!

Others of similar ilk were Seymour Price, a successful insurance broker who had given up his business to become General Manager and Secretary of the Baptist Insurance Society. He was chairman of the Ministerial Recognition Committee. Payne's fellow officers in the Baptist Union included Arnold Clark as Treasurer and Gordon Fairbairn as Solicitor. They supported Payne not least with monthly meetings of BU officers. The succession of Presidents was distinguished and supportive: H.R. Williamson, the experienced missionary and Overseas Secretary of the BMS, Arnold Clark, Henry Bonser - a remarkable and faithful area superintendent, Robert Child -Principal of Regent's Park College, Henry Cook, recently retired Superintendent of the Metropolitan Area, a pro-active Union servant and also deeply involved in European Baptist affairs, and Herbert Janes, a prosperous builder from Luton and generous supporter of Baptist causes. The President's office was viewed not as a sinecure nor just a twelve-month peripatetic ministry, but as helping to shoulder, as senior officer of the Union, the responsibilities for the well-being and spiritual prosperity of Baptists together. These Presidents brought their particular gifts to the office and were ready to become effective members of the team of officers. Payne encouraged this. The monthly meetings at the BU offices developed into a pattern of what today would be recognized as team leadership. It was, however, a team drawn not from within the Baptist Union staff but from the wider fellowship.

Although the election of the first woman as President of the Baptist Union was still twenty years in the future, the women's place in Union affairs was recognized and valued. Within the Church House Lois Chapple and Dorothy Finch were effective and loyal members of staff, with the former deeply involved in the wider world of the Baptist Women's League. On the Baptist Union Council Mrs Ernest Brown, Gwenyth Hubble, Principal of Carey Hall in Birmingham, Mrs H.H. Pewtress and Mrs O.D. Wiles were valued and participating members.

Another aspect of team leadership which Payne fostered immediately was his contact with the Superintendents Board. Its chairman was the Revd Sidney Morris who possessed outstanding pastoral gifts and a deep concern for the well-being of the ministers and churches. For thirty years he had ministered at Upper Holloway in London before becoming General Superintendent of the Southern Area in 1931, and then the Metropolitan Area 1934-39. His wisdom and experience had moulded the Board into an impressive and united team. Payne made time to be present at meetings of the Board, at least for part of the time, and evidently valued Superintendents as essential allies in the development of Baptists together. From time to time he referred to them as the 'diaconate' of the Union.

These informal and formal groupings which Payne developed were all part of his own perception of how he saw the Union developing in the 1950s and beyond. Shakespeare had created, Aubrey had consolidated, now Payne believed his task was to make clear to the members of associations, churches and colleges what it really meant to be Baptists together in mission.

He had received a 'text' from Aubrey's legacy. For within the 1951 Council Report the following comment occurs:

> Nothing has been more pleasing than to see the old rather official and stand-off relations between Churches and Associations on the one hand, and the Church House on the other, change into those of confidence and friendliness and easier approach so that those of us who work at the centre find ourselves borne along by a current of good will and common purpose.

While the cynic might say there was an element of wishful thinking and literary rhetoric in this, there is little doubt but that the statement contained a good measure of truth. The six years of the Second World War and its very difficult aftermath had helped to pressurize Baptists into mutual methodology for the common good. There was a growingly widespread recognition that Baptists needed to act and speak together.

This context made it all the more important for Payne to be assured of the support of all sections of the denomination. Sadly this ideal suffered a severe blow when on 23 March 1951, just a month before Payne took office, Percy Evans died suddenly. The loss was very serious to the denomination in general, but for Payne in particular the blow was devastating. As he wrote years later, 'the sky darkened for many that day'. Evans had been very persuasive in bringing Payne into office; he had assured him of his personal support and help. Evans would have facilitated contacts with those aspects of denominational life of which Payne had experienced little. Not surprisingly, when Payne responded to the denomination's welcome to him at the

Assembly he commented that, as he had anticipated the future, he had been tempted to run away from it and never more so than when he heard of the death of Percy Evans.

As it turned out, Evans was not the only loss of promised support that Payne suffered during his early years of office. Among others, in 1951 J.W. Ewing, R. Wilson Black and H.L. Taylor all died, and between 1952 and 1954 P.T. Thomson, S.W. Hughes and C.T. Le Quesne.

Nevertheless, Payne settled down to the task of making the associations and churches see and feel themselves together as the Union, as a visible fellowship in relationship with one another. The local church was the place where the universal church was made manifest. In 1948, Payne had helped to draft a statement, *The Baptist Doctrine of the Church*. The document was a substantial re-drafting - indeed, a rewriting - of the 1926 Reply of the Baptist Union Annual Assembly to the Lambeth Conference *Appeal to All Christian People*. The 1948 statement reflected Payne's views, later expressed in his book, *The Fellowship of Believers* (1952). The statement recorded:

> Although each local church is held to be competent under Christ to rule its own life, Baptists throughout their history have been aware of the perils of isolation and have sought safeguards against exaggerated individualism. From the seventeenth century there have been 'Associations' of Baptist Churches which sometimes appointed 'Messengers'; more recently their fellowship with one another has been greatly strengthened by the Baptist Union, the Baptist Missionary Society and the Baptist World Alliance. Indeed, we believe that a local church lacks one of the marks of a truly Christian community if it does not seek the fellowship of other Baptist churches.....

Payne believed that between the local church and the great concept of the universal church there had to be some form of manifestation of fellowship in order that the church might not only benefit from the mutuality of harmonious relationships but also function efficiently. He believed that the Baptist Union was one such manifestation. His concern was not, as Baptist apprehension has often judged, to create a hierarchy within the Union to dominate local churches. His conviction was that the Union was a community of the churches existing for their mutual benefit. To do this he believed that the issue was not simply structural but that the denomination should develop a functional ecclesiology of the Union as a foundation of effective interdependence. During his years in office he tried to expedite such a concept.

There is little doubt that he made progress in this policy. During his years in office communication possibilities improved and awareness of the Union grew apace amongst the churches. So did awareness of each other amongst both churches and ministers. This made the measure of diversity within the Union more evident: the more we are together, the more diverse we seem to be. Payne endeavoured to emphasize the benefits of such diversity without minimizing the inherent difficulties. His policy was to stress the importance for realistic interdependence of the diversities themselves. Unity in diversity was the policy. Payne used often to remind people that both Billy Graham and Martin Luther King were Baptists. The diversity of Baptists was not something to be regretted but something to be rejoiced in and to cope with, within an overall framework of unity. That, however, was not easily maintained; for example, the exploration in Alec Gilmore's collection of essays, *The Pattern of the Church* (1963), prompted the Baptist Revival Fellowship to produce *Liberty in the Lord*, questioning the direction of this new thinking.

Ernest Payne maintained a careful stewardship of the Baptist Union Council and its committee structures. He encouraged the appointment of younger folk and of women on to the committees by the then commonly used co-option procedures. He sought to ensure that there was a sensible balance on the Council itself, seeking to bring in 'new blood' whilst retaining 'elder statesmen', or at least those who in older age could contribute to the future and were not trapped in the past. He found inevitably from time to time that he, who was a formidable 'poacher' in the BU estates of the 1930s, became cast in the role of gamekeeper of the 1950s and 1960s, seeking to control the 'poachers' by the tactical methodology of recruiting the more vociferous as 'assistant gamekeepers'. He handled the Council with considerable diplomatic skill. He tried always as Secretary to claim the final word in any significant debate, summing up the various points of view with succinct wisdom and more often than not enabling the Council to arrive at a balanced compromise, representing the unity which could be expressed within the diversity. His policy accepted the inevitability of pragmatism but he never allowed pragmatism to become a principle in its own right. Whilst he was sometimes annoyed at what was said - and just occasionally rattled - he rarely showed such emotions. He personified a line in Kipling's poem, 'If': 'if you can keep your head when all about you are losing theirs and blaming it on you': every twentieth-century General Secretary from J.H. Shakespeare to David Coffey, could all too easily identify such situations within the Baptist Union Council!

The Baptist Union Council had noted in 1956 that the Ter-Jubilee of the Union would occur in 1962 and asked that a scheme for its worthy celebration be drawn up. The scheme was Payne's brainchild. He saw this as an opportunity for fostering still further and illustrating in practical terms what it meant to speak of Baptists together. The scheme as finally agreed by Council had three main emphases:

1) *Commemoration* It was to be an opportunity to inform and renew interest amongst all sections of the denomination in the history and principles of Baptists and the relevance of those two issues in the present.

2) *Evangelism* The churches needed to be called to prayer and action in new outreach and to be helped in carrying through a programme of sustained evangelism.

3) *Giving and Sharing* A sum of £300,000 should be raised, to be divided into four equal parts to

   i) augment the Loan Fund which assisted churches to develop through low interest loans
   ii) assist ministerial training by grants to the colleges and bursaries though the Scholarship Fund
   iii) augment the capital of the Home Work Fund
   iv) for the expenses of the celebration, the balance to be held for distribution to meet urgent needs prevailing at the close of the celebration.

The celebrations were to conclude with the Assembly of 1963.

Appropriate committees were set up in 1959 to prepare the way. The evangelism emphasis was put into the hands of the Evangelism Committee of the Union under the chairmanship of the Revd Hubert Janisch. It set about recalling the denomination to its missionary responsibilities; gave new thought to the nature of the gospel message and the context in which it was delivered; and called for the nurture and training of all church members, deploying a pamphlet entitled *A Spiritual Check-Up* as an aid in that. A literature subcommittee was set up under the chairmanship of J.O. Barrett, and one on finance under Arnold S. Clark, the Treasurer of the Union.

The literature sub-committee was remarkably active. The most significant publication was Payne's, *The Baptist Union: A Short History* (1959), which covered the first 150 years of the Union's life with remarkable comprehensiveness without being a mere catalogue. It remains an essential reference book. In addition, thirty-one Ter-Jubilee booklets were produced, all with a professionally designed uniform cover. All were sold at a subsidized price and they covered spirituality, evangelism, Christian education, Baptist history and principles, and explanations of the need for the financial appeal - to mention but a few. Astonishingly (for Baptists!) over 1,000,000 copies were printed, with a circulation beyond the denomination at home and amongst Baptists overseas. One or two continued in circulation long after the Ter-Jubilee celebrations concluded, notably a *Pocket History of Baptists* and *Baptist Principles* which continued in print with updated versions for more than thirty years. Beyond the denominationally-funded imprints, there were other publications of significance, including the much-acclaimed *Orders and Prayers for Church Worship* of E.A. Payne and Stephen Winward (1960), representing a more thoughtful approach to worship, and Alec Gilmore's *Christian Baptism* (1959), which set the debate about baptism within a deeper theological context.

A significant occasion was the calling of a denominational conference at Swanwick, Derbyshire, from 23 to 26 May 1961, the first event of its kind, although there had been conferences of the Men's Movement and the Women's Department for many years. The denominational conference sought to bring together a cross-section of the whole of Baptist life. To this Ter-Jubilee Conference 271 delegates came. Each association had been invited to choose representatives proportional to its numerical strength, including ministerial and lay, men and women, young and old. Each college sent a staff member and a student. All the General Superintendents attended, as did delegations from the BMS and the Scottish and Welsh Unions. There was no set detailed agenda, no 'directive' or manifesto from Baptist Church House. The delegates came to worship, listen and talk. There was little atmosphere of complacency, simply an attempt at realism in tackling the general theme which was, quite simply, the Baptist denomination as it was at home and abroad in 1961. It was hoped that the Holy Spirit would be allowed free rein amongst the delegates. Much of the time was spent in groups. As it turned out, the statement which emerged was, perhaps inevitably, a frank assessment of Baptists together as perceived in 1961. In brief, there were seven sections to the Statement which were generally agreed and of which quotations at length are made here only from the first two. It is incidentally interesting to note how many of the themes of the Denominational Conference at Swanwick were echoed three decades later at the Denominational Consultation at Swanwick in 1996.

The foundation section of the Statement said this:

1) The independency which has characterized the outlook and practice of many, if not all, of our churches in the last 100 years, needs now to be supplemented by a much clearer realization of the necessity of their interdependency in fellowship, not only on practical grounds but in the light of the New Testament and any true doctrine of the church based thereon. The meaning of this (implicit in Baptist principles and clearly expressed in seventeenth-century Confessions) for our denominational life, needs immediate study, that practical steps for manifesting our true unity in Christ may be agreed upon and put into effect.

2) There was unanimous agreement on the importance of the Associations for the healthy development of our denominational life on the grounds of both history and present experience. Some feeling was expressed that it might be wise to consider the re-drawing of certain boundaries, the development of smaller district units and the importance of securing truly representative character of Association Committees.

3) Various questions relating to the ministry of the church were raised and discussed. The fundamental ministry is that of the total membership together of every church enabled by a ministry of those called to special forms of service. Issues raised in that latter context included ministerial settlement and removal, the recognition and ordination of those over forty, the distinction (if any) between full and part-time ministry, increments for length of service and the need for greater support and encouragement of lay preachers.

4) The need for experimentation and pilot schemes in developing church life for mission, including larger church groups in town and in countryside and the parallel use of team ministry. Particular concern was expressed for village churches.

5) The need for *sustained* teaching both before and after baptism with the possible use of 'teaching' missions and including the need for books and booklets for new church members.

6) The appointment of commissions to prepare reports on a number of these issues was suggested, with reports being widely disseminated amongst Association and church meetings.

7) The need was emphasized for Baptists to be more aware of the wider situation - notably of Baptists throughout the world in

alliance. Lack of knowledge often contributed to misunderstandings of that wider situation - including the so-called 'Ecumenical Movement'.

When the Ter-Jubilee came to its end in 1963 the £300,000 fell short by some £10,000. But as the expenses were below those allowed for in the original budget for the celebrations, the distribution of the money from the so-called 'fourth quarter' was not adversely affected.

A fuller aspect of Payne's concern for Baptists together was revealed in his involvement in the work of the Baptist World Alliance. The year 1955 saw the fiftieth anniversary of its foundation, beginning as it did in London on 5 July 1905 under the Presidency of Alexander Maclaren, one of the foremost preachers amongst English Baptists. Maclaren reminded the congregation of 'two crystal phrases' which were 'in the name of Christ' and 'by the power of the Spirit'. He then went on to say, 'I should like that there be no misunderstanding on the part of the English public, or the American public either, before whom we are taking a prominent position, for a day at any rate, as to where we stand in the continuity of the historic Church ..... as a simple acknowledgement of where we stand and what we believe would you rise to your feet and following the lead of your President, would you repeat the Apostles' Creed - will you?' The whole gathered company did just that.

No such remarkable affirmation marked the beginning of the Golden Jubilee Congress of the BWA. But the Archbishop of Canterbury, Geoffrey Fisher, welcomed the delegates impressively at the opening session. A total of 8,524 delegates registered for the Congress which, in spite of early apprehensions, turned out to be a very successful event, not least because its finances ended up with a considerable surplus. Present at the Congress was a strong delegation from the Soviet Union. Vivid memories remain. The Albert Hall was packed to capacity for an evening pageant, 'And there's another country', written and produced by the Revd Arthur Davies, then minister of Salter's Hall in London. There is a story (said to be true!) of one disgruntled overseas visitor who threatened to draw a gun on the manager of the Albert Hall in a fruitless attempt to get in. The final rally was at the Arsenal Football Ground and was addressed memorably by Dr Billy Graham. The whole celebration confirmed the tremendous potential that Baptists have when they work together in mission and testimony. Payne was well satisfied!

The organizational responsibility had been shared, notably between O.D. Wiles at the Baptist Church House and Alec A. Wilson at the BMS, largely co-ordinated by a gifted layman, Ronald Bell. This close BU/BMS co-operation stimulated yet again the issue of Baptists together illustrated in the relationship of the Union and the BMS.

After the 1955 Congress the Union Council and the General Committee of the BMS had agreed a joint declaration of intent to deal seriously with their relationships. Payne, therefore, drafted a memorandum indicating various alternative procedures for re-opening the issue. When the 1938 Russell Square scheme was under discussion, Payne, then at the BMS, had much sympathy with it and felt that the Assembly session which, in effect, rejected the scheme was never allowed to hear the whole story nor to consider the issue impartially. He was disappointed at the outcome not only from his personal viewpoint but because he believed that, on the whole, the denomination desired to see much closer relations, not least in shared headquarters. The response of the BMS Home Secretary to Payne's memorandum was, in his view, disappointing in its coolness. No further progress was made.

When re-appointed in 1956 for another five years, Payne re-iterated his concern on this issue in his acceptance speech. Speaking of the need for closer togetherness of the two organizations, he observed:

> Five years ago I should have said this was mainly necessary because of the denominational situation in this country. That is still important, but I am now convinced that it is a situation of our missionary churches overseas and the prospects facing them that make it urgent and imperative. I do not see clearly what to do. But both bodies have pledged themselves to give their minds to this question. I hope it can be done with restraint, sympathy, and mutual confidence.

In fact, his hopes were not to be fulfilled in his lifetime. During the 1960s joint officers' meetings of the Society and the Baptist Union had been widened to include the officers of the separate Baptist Unions of Scotland and Wales. Whilst this, in a proper sense, was a further manifestation of Baptists together, it had the effect of complicating discussion between the Baptist Union at Southampton Row, and the BMS at Gloucester Place, for it was a reminder that the Baptist Missionary Society had a commitment wider than simply to the Baptist Union of Great Britain, for the Society worked also with and was dependent for support on the other two Unions. During the 1960s these Unions grew more conscious of their independence, linked in some way - whether consciously or not - with inherent nationalism, especially in Scotland.

Nevertheless, in 1961 the Baptist Union Assembly passed

enthusiastically a resolution proposed by Ernest Payne and seconded by J.B. Middlebrook which said:

> This Assembly gives Council full authority, jointly with the Baptist Missionary Society, to build or acquire premises which, in the opinion of the Council, will be suitable as denominational headquarters. The general aim should be to make provision for the present and estimated future requirements of the Union and the Baptist Missionary Society and such other organizations and activities as may be conveniently housed or conducted in the same building or buildings.

A similar resolution was passed by the BMS members' meeting, being moved by J.B. Middlebrook and seconded by Payne.

But apart from a serious attempt, which proved abortive, to devise an acceptable and viable scheme based on developing the site of the Beechen Grove Church in Watford, and one or two other false trails, no further progress was made on fulfilling the terms of such resolutions. It was not until nearly a quarter of a century later, in 1989, that the 1961 resolution was implemented. By then Payne had been dead for nearly ten years.

Payne's ecumenical attitude was well known. It was not only Baptists who needed to manifest a sense of belonging together: so did the wider church. The story of Baptist involvement ecumenically in the twentieth century requires separate treatment. It must suffice here to emphasize that Payne was a known supporter of ecumenicity when he was first appointed. In so electing him the denomination tacitly acknowledged that it was open to such developments. In fairness, it should be said that, in spite of dissenting voices, the Union Assembly has remained supportive of such a stance throughout the second half of this century. Baptists have played - and still play - a significant role in developing church relations.

In September 1964 the First British Faith and Order Conference was held at Nottingham. All participating churches were asked to respond to its findings. The Baptist Union Council of November 1964 first referred the Nottingham request to the Advisory Committee for Church Relations which produced in March 1965 an interim reply and was then urged by Council to prepare a comprehensive statement for the guidance of the churches. The outcome was the report, *Baptists and Unity*, which remains still, somewhat dated though it be, the most comprehensive general statement on the subject produced by the Union this century. Although a group of ministers and lay folk were entrusted to produce the Report, there was naturally enough close contact with Payne as Secretary of the Union and experienced ecumenist.

Just one paragraph from the Report is a fair reflection of how the majority of Baptists viewed ecumenism in the 1960s.

> ..... the visible unity of Christ's church is a concept rooted in the New Testament and we cannot, as true followers of Christ, ignore what the Spirit is doing in the churches today. Do any of us really believe that it is not the Spirit of Christ who is drawing churches out of isolation in to discussion and activity together? The realities of the Church's unity that have engaged our attention surely demand some effort to be made to embody them in the empirical life of the church; is it really God's will to cease such efforts and leave the appalling *status quo* to the Second Coming of Christ and the Last Judgement? And what will the Judge say to us if we do?

The Report was adopted by the March Council of 1967 and sent to the churches for their study and comments. A revised document, based on the responses from the churches, entitled *Baptists and Unity Reviewed*, was presented to the Assembly in 1969 and endorsed by 1,125 votes to 356. By that time Payne had been two years retired. But he was content with the outcome!

At the beginning of February 1958 Ronald Thomson had joined the staff of the Union as Assistant General Secretary. The adjective is important to note. In 1948 O.D. Wiles had been appointed as Deputy General Secretary just before Aubrey indicated his intention to retire in 1951. Wiles was a good and competent servant of the Union but in the proper sense of the word he was not Aubrey's 'Deputy'. In Aubrey's absence it was not assumed that he was 'deputy' in the sense of assuming the Secretary's 'mantle'. He assisted Aubrey effectively in a number of ways, but he did not formally deputize. Payne was meticulous in his use of language, some might say to the point of pedantry. But it was important for people to know where they were, who they were and what was expected of them.

The appointment of Thomson as Payne's assistant admirably suited Thomson's gifts. He was an excellent administrator, a meticulous minute taker and had the gift of patience to listen and wisdom to advise. He was also aware of the developing technology of the 1950s and 1960s, particularly in communications. One of his first activities was to update the whole telephone network in the Church House and to install proper 'intercom' facilities.

Thomson was a Regent's man of the early 1930s and had been in pastorates for twenty-seven years. In his retirement he wrote a journal recording his childhood in London in the early decades of the twentieth century and also reflecting at some length on his time in Baptist Church House. He functioned as Secretary of the Psalms and Hymns Trust from 1958 to 1977 and succeeded his predecessor in chaplaincy involvement. O.D. Wiles, who during his army service had been Deputy Chaplain General, had acted as Organizing Secretary of the United Navy, Army and Air Force Board which in 1914, largely as a result of pressure from J.H. Shakespeare, had been formally constituted by the Armed Services to secure appointments of Navy, Army and RAF chaplains to care for those in the services who came from Baptist, Congregational and Methodist backgrounds. It was this responsibility which Thomson inherited when Wiles retired.

Part of the developing Union methodology which Thomson notes during Payne's time was the Baptist use of commissions. J.H. Shakespeare had tended to act without broad consultation. Not surprisingly, because the Baptist Union Council of his day, significant though it was, did not overmuch preoccupy itself with detailed general theological issues, only with how they effected the practical outworking of the denomination's life. Aubrey recognized the growing need for wide consultation as the concept of Baptists together became of increased significance to the Associations and churches. So commissions began - and developed apace. In 1936 'the Committee on Baptist Polity' had been set up, but it was not until 1942 that it finally reported. In 1944 the 'State of the Churches' was discussed in preparation for the longed-for return of peace.

In Payne's time the movement accelerated, prompted further to a considerable degree by the statement from the Jubilee Conference at Swanwick mentioned earlier. There was, to name but a few, a report on *The Meaning and Practice of Ordination among Baptists* (48 pages, 1957), a report on *The Doctrine of the Ministry* (46 pages, 1961), *The Report of the Commission on the Associations* (57 pages, 1964), a report on *The Child and the Church* (1966), and *Baptists and Unity* (60 pages, 1967). Thomson remarks somewhat ruefully: 'We had got into the habit of setting up commissions every time a problem came up for which there did not seem an obvious solution'. There is a large measure of truth in that statement. On the other hand the Commission had the merit of recording denominational thinking on major issues, of providing a document for discussion and of, albeit in a somewhat haphazard way, initiating thinking, possibilities, and ideas and developments which over the years found their way into denominational practice. There is, of course, the inherent danger that if not immediately implemented such reports are shelved and in later days referred back to all too infrequently so that the wheel is being constantly re-invented.

In May 1965 Payne wrote to the President of the Baptist Union, Dr Howard Williams, indicating that when his third term of service ended in Spring 1966 he would be within a year of his sixty-fifth birthday and that it had been always his intention to retire at that age. He was invited to continue until August 1967. The wisdom of his decision to retire was confirmed when, at the end of March 1967, he suffered a heart attack more severe than his previous one in 1958. But in spite of initial uncertainty, he recovered sufficiently to be back at work by the early summer, though he found the last year of office increasingly trying.

The final Council Report of his secretaryship should be read in full by anyone who seeks to discover Payne's thoughts as he came to retirement. Time and again what are evidently his personal reflections on the denomination are but thinly disguised. His deep concern for the life and witness of Baptists together is clearly evident. This is particularly true of the concluding paragraphs where reference is made to a report in *The Times* newspaper of 19 December 1966. This commented: 'In a way it is courageous of the Bishop of Chester, Chairman of the Church of England's Committee on the Ordination of Women to admit that the fact of people's prejudice, however right or wrong in theory, is a humanly relevant factor in the case. At least this avoids the danger of hypocrisy, which more dogmatic assertions do not.' Council's Report then says:

> The Council believes that these words from *The Times* are words it would be well for Baptists to ponder and apply to their own situation. They have reference to the question of the right 'Baptist' attitude to closer relations with other traditions ..... to the relation of local churches to one another and to the Union ..... to the Baptist Union and the Baptist Missionary Society. During the year little or no progress has been made towards a joint headquarters, or the more important matter of closer integration of the activities and structures of the two bodies ..... and to the relations of individual Baptists to one another when they differ in theological emphasis, in social behaviour and in political judgement. Our point of reference should be the revolutionary love and vision of Christ. It is in His light that we shall see light.

These words proved prophetic as the story of Baptists together over the final decades of this century unfolded.

Payne's retirement lasted nearly thirteen years. They were active years with his involvement in the World Council of Churches continuing until December 1975. Then in 1976 he was elected to the vice-presidency of the Baptist Union. When approached about the nomination he was hesitant in the extreme. He consulted widely and in the end accepted the nomination which came unanimously from the March Council of 1975. His own fears were never completely allayed but he agreed to stand. So he came to serve the denomination as an officer again from 1976 to 1979. Beyond retirement he thus had a considerable part still to play in the life of Council and denomination and therefore of Baptists Together. On Monday, 14 January 1980, he died suddenly at the Bonnington Hotel in Southampton Row.

R.W. Thomson who knew Payne well and worked closely with him for nine years includes in his unpublished memoir (which is quoted here with the author's permission) these words:

> Dr Payne deserves a greater tribute than I can pen. He and I never had a cross word throughout all my time with him ..... I know that many both in the Baptist Church House and outside found him somewhat cold and aloof. One had to know him well to realize the warm heart that beat beneath the withdrawn manner ..... Each morning the heads of departments (there were then many more than three!) met for coffee for half an hour, if we could draw him out on some subject he would sit for much longer and chat in the most charming and enthralling way ..... One of his most endearing habits was to ask me early in the week where I was preaching on Sunday. He would wish me well ..... and later in the week he would hand me a slip of paper - usually the back of an old envelope on which he would have scribbled some interesting story concerned with the church or one of its ministers - always something newsworthy. It made a great difference to be able to include this in what one had to say, the church felt that the Union really did take a personal interest in it ..... J.H. Shakespeare made the denomination what it is today but it was Ernest Payne who showed how it could and should be held together. He commented one day, somewhat ruefully, 'The Almighty has bestowed on us a more than generous share of enthusiastic people - but they are a varied company!'

THE CHILD AND THE CHURCH
A Baptist Perspective

I

On 5 September 1524 Conrad Grebel, leader of the Zürich radical reforming group, wrote to Thomas Müntzer, the German radical, indicating his group's intention on biblical grounds of moving from the practice of infant baptism to that of believers. In so doing they recognized that the question of the child and the church required to be faced. Their answer was clear and simple.

> We hold that all children who have not yet come to the discernment of good and evil and have not yet eaten of the tree of knowledge, that they are surely saved by the suffering of Christ, the new Adam ..... but they are not yet grown up into the infirmity of our broken nature - unless indeed it can be proved that Christ did not suffer for children.[1]

What the Zürich Anabaptist group subsequently did about their children, apart from refusing to baptize them, is not clear. But we do know that on 16 January 1525 Balthasar Hubmaier, who shared Conrad Grebel's view, wrote from Waldshut to Oecolampadius, the reformer in Basel, describing his practice concerning infants.

> Instead of baptism, I have the church come together, bring the infant in, explain in German the gospel, 'they brought little children' (Matthew 19). When a name is given it, the whole church prays for the child on bended knees and commends it to Christ, that he will be gracious and intercede for it. But if the parents are still weak, and positively wish that the child be baptized then I baptize it; and I am weak with the weak for the time being until they can be better instructed.[2]

How far the sixteenth-century Anabaptists are directly related to the English Baptists of the following century remains still an open question. Nevertheless, when John Smyth and his group of English Separatists broke with the Anglican Church, including its practice of infant baptism, they

---

[1] *Spiritual and Anabaptist Writers* (Documents Illustrative of the Radical Reformation), edited by G.H. Williams and A.M. Mergal, Volume XXV, Library of Christian Classics, London 1957, p.81. Original letter in Stadtsbibliothek St Gall, Band XI 97.
[2] George H. Williams, *The Radical Reformation*, p.135.

realized also that the issue of the child and the church required to be faced.[3]

What was to be the status of children *vis-à-vis* the believing Christian community? Smyth's answer, like that of Conrad Grebel, was seemingly simple, if rather more theologically refined. He drew a distinction between sin as a state and sin as an act. Although Smyth is seen as a pioneer of the General Baptists, there was sufficient Calvinism in his thought to cause him what Michael Walker calls 'a partial agnosticism' as to the status of infants.[4] If an infant was elected, then baptism could not affect the issue one way or another until election could be made sure and evidenced, then baptism could be administered.

Smyth's colleague, Thomas Helwys, in his work *A Short and Plain Proof that no Infants are Condemned*[5] developed the distinction between original and actual sin. But sin is not solely a matter of individual responsibility for there is an involvement also of all humanity in the sin of Adam. But 'by grace Christ hath freed Adam and in him all mankind from that sin of Adam'. Helwys stresses that sin is a personal responsibility, but also that the death of Christ is for all. Christ's death is as far reaching in its effect as Adam's sin. An infant outside the sphere of moral responsibility and therefore outside the sphere of consenting sin is within the salvation won by the second Adam.[6]

Smyth and Helwys both appear simply to 'write large' the basic statement in Grebel's 1524 letter. Later in the seventeenth century Thomas Grantham, the General Baptist Messenger, returned to the theme in his *Christianismus Primitivus*.[7] He used the concept of Christ as the New Adam as the 'representative' figure of the covenant. God had made a covenant with Adam (Genesis 3:15) and this covenant had never been repealed. All infants, therefore, regardless of parentage, are members of the church by virtue of that covenant. For Grantham humankind does not stand outside the Body of Christ waiting to be gathered in. It is the Body of Christ *out of which* persons can sin themselves in the years of responsibility.[8]

---

[3] On this issue Baptist historians continue to be indebted to Dr M.J. Walker, see especially Michael J. Walker, 'The Relation of Infants to the Church, Baptism and Gospel in Seventeenth-Century Baptist Theology', *Baptist Quarterly* XXI, April 1966, pp.2-62.

[4] Walker, op.cit., p.246.

[5] ibid., p.247.

[6] ibid.

[7] T. Grantham, *Christianismus Primitivus*, 1678, 2nd Treatise, Pt II p.3.

[8] T. Grantham, *The Controversie Concerning Infants Church Membership Epitomized*, London 1680, p.46. See Walker, op.cit., p.250.

At the same time, however, he went on to maintain that the children of believers stood in a particular *relationship* to the visible church. It was a relationship of prayer and pastoral concern. Upon parents is laid the responsibility of bringing up their children in an atmosphere of family devotion. Grantham acknowledged that the children of believing parents are in a particular way 'related to the visible Church, being in a more visible state of Beatitude as being given to God in the Name of Christ from the womb'.[9]

A second, separate strain of Baptists with Calvinist views which emerged in London about 1616 faced the same issues. For them, the matter of the child and the church was closely related to the concept of the covenant. Israel was elected to be the people of God and so the church consists of the elect whom God has chosen by His grace. Children have a place in that covenant. The old covenant *prefigured* the new. For Calvin this had meant that as circumcision was the visible sign of entry into the old covenant so infant baptism was the sign of entry into the new. With this interpretation by Calvin, however, the Particular Baptists took issue. They did not deny that there was continuity between the old and new covenants but claimed that the old had to be interpreted in the light of the new. Christ is the expositor of Moses, not vice versa. Infant baptism makes 'the Old Testament expound the new, whereas the new should expound the old: Christ should and doth expound Moses'.[10]

Furthermore, whilst acknowledging the continuity of the covenants, they also drew attention to the discontinuity. The community of the old covenant was a racial group, the new covenant community was a multi-racial group called out of all the nations by grace. Response to that grace was by faith leading to baptism and entry into the church.

Nevertheless, the Particular Baptists also recognized that the infants of believers stood in a particular relationship to the church. John Tombes described the children of believers as being 'born in the bosom of the Church, of Godly parents, who by prayers, instruction, example will undoubtedly educate them in the true faith of Christ'.[11]

---

[9] T. Grantham, *The Controversie Concerning Infants Church Membership Epitomized*, London 1680, p.46. See Walker, op.cit., p.250.
[10] Paul Hobson, *The Fallacy of Infant Baptism Discovered*, London 1645.
[11] John Tombes, *Examen of the Sermon of Mr Stephen Marshall about Infant Baptism*, London 1645, pp.32-3.

What then of the *status* of infants? For Michael Walker depiction of the views of the Particular Baptists as one of 'optimistic agnosticism'[12] finds evidence in Christopher Blackwood who writes,

> the Scripture has not revealed to us anything clearly concerning the salvation or damnation of infants ..... It is most likely that infants, as well as others, are saved by the presentment of the satisfaction of Christ to God's justice for overall sin.[13]

Evidence is scanty as to how far the seventeenth-century Baptists practised any form of service for the child. Thomas Grantham, on the basis of the blessing of children by Jesus, stated that the children of believing parents are 'devoted to God by the prayers of the Church ..... and accordingly we do dedicate [them] to him from the womb'.[14] Paedobaptists, he suggested, 'should do to their infants as Christ did to them which were brought to him, either by praying for them themselves or by presenting them to Christ's Ministers that they might do it for them in the most solemn manner'.[15]

Clear evidence for some such practice is found in Bristol. In 1642 during the Civil War Thomas Ewins had come to Bristol together with his congregation from Llanvaches in Monmouthshire. He came to exercise a wide preaching and teaching ministry which included, from time to time, the church at Broadmead. Ewins recounts an occasion when a 'Godly' woman, one at whose husband's house the church often used to meet, 'was delivered of a child' and invited the church to meet at her house to render praise to God.

> Now when the church was met she decided that her children might be presented to the Lord by prayer, both that which she then lay with, and one more the age of two years ..... the like was done again about two years after when the Lord gave her another child, and as I have known it done in Wales.[16]

Ewins goes on to suggest that any 'godly woman', a member of a congregation, who has a child should present herself with her child in the church so that God may be praised and her child presented with prayer in dedication to God. The name of the child should be declared by the parents

---

[12] Walker, op.cit., p.258.
[13] Christopher Blackwood, *The Storming of Anti-Christ*, London 1644, p.11.
[14] *Christianismus Primitivus* BK II, p.6.
[15] ibid., see Walker p.250.
[16] *The Records of a Church of Christ in Bristol, 1640-1687*, ed. Roger Hayden, Bristol Record Society, 1974, p.53.

and the child's name should be entered

> into the book where the names of the congregation are written together with other dedicated children as the Children of the Church who upon occasion may be mentioned to the Lord as the seed of the faithful, that when the children come to age, and the Lord shall give them to profess Faith in Christ, and that they do believe with all their hearts as Acts 8:37 they may then be admitted to the Ordinances of Christ, both Baptism and the Lord's Supper as believers were in primitive times.[17]

Thus the return to the practice of believers' baptism on the basis of biblical practice and theology led the seventeenth-century Baptists to face two connected issues relating to the child and the church. The first was the status of the child theologically. This involved:

1) the claim that there is a distinction between sin as a state and sin as an act

2) the inclusion of children in the salvation achieved by Christ as the representative New Adam

3) for the Particular Baptists, the inclusion of the children of believers in the New Covenant in Christ

4) for the General Baptists, the claim that the children of believers are in a more visible state of Beatitude.

The second issue was the need for a service for children, certainly for children of the 'godly', in the midst of the congregation which would include prayers of thanksgiving, a prayer seeking God's blessing on the child, the naming of the child and the inclusion of the child's name in the Book of the Congregation. The intention was that, being now the children of the church, prayer would subsequently be offered regularly on their behalf in the anticipation that the process would lead to baptism, membership of the visible church and entry to the Lord's Supper.

Thus it is evident that there is ample support within our Baptist origins for seeing the child and the church as an essential issue in Baptist life and thought.

---

[17] Thomas Ewins, *The church of Christ in Bristol,* 1656, p.64a, quoted in T.L. Underwood, 'Child Dedication Services amongst British Baptists in the Seventeenth Century', *Baptist Quarterly* XXIII, October 1969, pp.165-9.

II

Relatively little research has been done thus far on Baptist attitudes and thought concerning the child and the church in the eighteenth and much of the nineteenth century. Two isolated references may be mentioned which indicate that the issue was still alive.

On 4 December 1753 there were twenty-three signatures to the new church covenant of Westgate Particular Baptist Church in Bradford. The seventh clause of the covenant reads, 'And as we have given our children to the Lord by a Solemn Dedication, so we will endeavour through divine help to teach them the way of the Lord and command them to keep it, setting before them a Holy example worthy of their imitation and continuing in prayer to God for their conversion and salvation.'[18]

Whilst there is no certainty that the 'Solemn Dedication' was one special occasion which took the form of a formal act of worship, the phraseology of the clause tends to suggest that this is the most natural interpretation of its meaning.

Adam Taylor, writing of the General Baptists, mentioned the Barton Preachers, an evangelical group who adopted the sentiments of the Baptists in 1755. In turning from infant baptism to believers' baptism, the group continued to bring infants to church for blessing.

> They brought their infants in the time of public service, to the minister; who, taking them in his arms pronounced an affectionate benediction on them using ..... Aaron's words, from Numbers 6:24-27 ..... Suitable admonition to the parents and earnest and affectionate prayer for them and their offspring concluded the solemn and interesting transaction.[19]

In the final decades of the nineteenth century, however, the issue clearly re-emerges in Baptist thought and practice.

In 1858 John Clifford, aged twenty-two, settled at Praed Street Chapel in London. Charles Bateman, writing in 1904, commented,

> His [John Clifford's] belief in immersion does not prevent his adopting a Dedication Service in addition. This he uses because of the fact that many of his people - like Congregationalists - desire to associate their children with the church and seek its prayers, just after

---

[18] Covenant quoted in *Baptist Quarterly* XIX July 1962, pp.289-91.
[19] Adam Taylor, *History of English General Baptists*, London 1818, 180 Vol II, p.29f.

their birth. He has told me that at first his wife and himself, when they settled at Praed Street, visited the homes of the members and there conducted the Dedication Service. He afterwards found that the Church, which is of a cosmopolitan character and includes Methodists and Congregationalists, as well as Baptists, desired a public service so that the members could take part in it.[20]

When Charles Williams of Accrington produced *The Principles and Practices of the Baptists* in 1879, there was no mention of a dedication service, even though he discusses the Baptist view of the status of the child. When the second edition was published in 1903, a dedication service was included but the author felt it wise to include what he calls 'a word of explanation' as to its purpose.[21] This suggests that it was something of an innovation. Williams writes:

> Many families desire more than individual thanksgiving for preserving the life of the mother and for the child. Not unnaturally they wish their pastor to lead them alike in praise for the preservation of life and for the gift of life and in prayer for the mother and her babe. In the circumstances certain Baptist ministers accept the invitation to be present at a family service for this purpose.[22]

For their use a form of service was suggested which contained a number of biblical texts, including Psalm 103:1-5 and 13-14; Psalm 127:3-5a; Deuteronomy 6:4-7; Mark 10: 14-16; a selection from I Samuel 2 and 3; Isaiah 40: 11ff. The rubric which followed the suggested scripture said, 'The Service should close with praise for "goodness and mercy" shown to the mother, and with prayer in which the child is consecrated to the service of the Saviour and is commended to His guardianship and guidance'.

In 1905 the Kingsgate Press published *A Manual for Free Church Ministers*, compiled by G.P. Gould and J.H. Shakespeare. It began the pattern of Infant Dedication which became increasingly used in Baptist

---

[20] Charles T. Bateman, *John Clifford: Free Church Leader and Preacher*, London 1904, p.77.

[21] Charles Williams, *The Principles and Practices of the Baptists*, London 2nd edition 1903. For this and other help in this section, I am grateful to the Revd Dr Anthony Cross who is engaged upon significant research on Baptism amongst Baptists in the twentieth century.

[22] Op.cit., p.113.

churches during the first half of the twentieth century. The opening rubric stated, 'The Dedication Service usually follows the regular Morning Service'.[23] The meaning and intention of the dedication is threefold:

- to give thanks to God for the precious gift of the child,
- to bring the child to God as an act of consecration,
- to take solemn vows to train the child in the 'fear and nurture of the Lord'.

Scripture passages were to be read from Old and New Testament. These echoed those suggested by Charles Williams and are followed by a suggested brief address in which the child is described as one 'coming out of the unseen; born into a redeemed world; for whom the Saviour died; and called, therefore, by divine mercy to the inheritance of eternal life'. The parents are reminded that 'You are entering on a solemn responsibility, too great for any to bear alone ..... you will need continual grace and wisdom to guide the child into the ways of truth and goodness'.

Reading the second half of the address, one cannot help but be struck by the recurring emphasis on the discipline of the life opening up for the child of ninety years ago.

> These little hands will, perhaps, in days to come, have to bear heavy burdens; these little feet may have to tread a hard way. But at least it is possible for you in these early years to soothe and gladden, to cheer and bless.
>
> We do not travel far in life before we learn that all our joy is touched with pain and that sorrow sometimes strikes us through our tenderest and holiest relationships.[24]

There followed a prayer to God, the Source of all life, for the home, the parents, the child - particularly that 'this child may be brought to know and love Thee in Jesus Christ and may yield to Thy governance and find delight in doing Thy will'. The service concluded, with the parents standing, being asked the child's name and the minister, using the name given, pronouncing the Blessing from Numbers 6:24-26 and the Grace. There is no mention of

---

[23] *A Manual for Free Church Ministers*, compiled by G.P. Gould and J.H. Shakespeare, Kingsgate Press, London, n.d. but 1905. The final section contains eight hymns judged suitable for the various services contained in the manual. The suggested hymn for the Dedication is 'Standing forth on life's rough way'.

[24] op.cit. p.36.

the minister taking the child into his own arms.

The practice was not universally accepted. That there were those who viewed Dedication Services as unscriptural and therefore undesirable is evidenced from a discussion in 1908 in the correspondence column of the *Baptist Times & Freeman*.[25]

By 1911, however, the *Fraternal*, the magazine of the Baptist Ministers Fraternal Union, was publishing a 'Form of Service for the Dedication of Infants' by J.H. Rushbrooke.[26] An editorial footnote cautiously recorded that it was published 'At the request of several brethren, as a form which has, in some degree, commended itself in use, and may possibly be suggestive to those who are instituting similar services. Criticism or correspondence upon the subject will be welcomed.' It is worthy of note that the editor was none other than J.H. Rushbrooke himself!

The introduction to Rushbrooke's service order is important in that it introduces, not only the significance of the service for the child and its parents, but also 'for the members of the Christian Society with which these are associated and the congregation now present'. For closely and personally as the service concerns the parents and the children, *'it could have no rightful place in the public worship of God at the accustomed hour of common praise and prayer unless it likewise concerned the Church which has its home here'* [my italics. WMSW]. Thus the ecclesiological dimension of the dedication service is deemed an essential element. Indeed, the Church of Jesus is the instrument of the Kingdom of God,

> the representative of the Lord Jesus Christ, charged with the continuance of His work in His spirit, and therefore bound to adopt His attitude towards all, including those who, by reason of their tender age, are not yet consciously His disciples and are incapable of receiving baptism upon a profession of personal faith.[27]

After reading Mark 10: 13-16, the minister says 'the congregation assembled today, a portion of the Church of the Lord Jesus, expresses in His name His welcome of the little children', and continues, 'the family aspect of our Church life is prominent in this dedication service'. In this context the church gathered in worship is bound to the family and child at the centre of

---

[25] *Baptist Times and Freeman*, 7 August 1908, p.556.
[26] *The Fraternal* Vol.V, 2, June 1911, pp.42-7.
[27] Ibid., p.43.

the service. But the dedicatory act is personal to the family in their thanksgiving, recognition of their responsibility and need for Divine help. After further exhortation and scripture quotation the parents are invited to stand and then the minister says, 'And I ask all present, who desire to express the welcome of Christ to this little one and to associate themselves with these parents in thanksgiving and in prayer likewise to rise in their places'.[28] A prayer then followed, ending with the blessing from Numbers 6:24-26 and then a hymn and the Benediction.

The editorial request for criticism or correspondence seems not to have produced any response. But looking back now, we can see that this form of Rushbrooke's was a further significant step in the developing pattern of the dedication service.

Clearly there was a gradual process of acceptance amongst the Baptist churches of a dedication service. But many still doubted. Their hesitation sprang from the lack of clear biblical evidence for such a service and a fear of it being in any way viewed as related to infant baptism. In 1915 Mrs Charles Brown penned 'A plea for the General Adoption of an Infant Dedication Service in our Churches'. 'It seems astonishing that we consecrate marriage and death by religious services, yet when children are born to us, because we do not hold baptism to be appropriate, we have in the past dispensed with a religious service altogether'. She pointed out the pastoral need and evangelical opportunity of such service: 'Dedication Services furnish a real opportunity for reaching the hearts of parents at a time when they are especially tender and susceptible of influence'.[29]

Doubts remained. In 1925 F.C. Spurr, in the series *A Baptist Apologetic for Today*,[30] wrote, 'It is only within recent years that the solemn service of the Dedication of Infants has come into use amongst us. And there are still many who look askance at it.' Spurr's contribution was headed 'Our Present, Positive Message'. He argued that discipleship is the fundamental condition for church membership and on the basis of this concept talked about the position of the child of Christian parents.

> And just as every English child is treated as a potential citizen so every child of Christian parents should be treated as a potential citizen of the Kingdom of God. Many Baptists have failed to grasp this elementary

---

[28] ibid., p.46.
[29] *Baptist Times and Freeman*, 30 July 1915.
[30] *Baptist Times*, 5 November 1925.

truth. They have treated their children as 'outsiders' waiting for the mysterious breath of God to quicken them. If we are to take Christ seriously, we ought to dedicate our children. Dedication, however, is not baptism and ought not to be confounded with it .....

> When the child is grown and educated in the things of Christ, then the heart being willingly surrendered to Him, is the time for Baptism ..... Baptism should respect discipleship and discipleship alone. The infant dedication *and a later ratification in baptism* [author's italics] is on the lines of the New Testament.[31]

Here was a Baptist in 1925 beginning to argue along the lines of what today is called 'Christian Initiation'. He went on to suggest that for some paedobaptists infant baptism was nothing more than infant dedication so he argued that this line of thought should be persistently taught to our own people. But we ought also to witness this to our fellow Evangelicals who confound dedication and baptism. So 'why not retain the dedication and defer the baptism until it becomes an intelligent act on the part of the subject? .....'[32] The apologetic for Infant Dedication was properly beginning to have an ecumenical edge.

The Baptist response accepted at the 1926 Union Assembly to the 'Appeal to all Christian People', issued by the 1920 Lambeth Conference, contained no such courageous edge. It limited its words on the child and the church to safer parameters:

> In our judgement the baptism of infants incapable of offering a personal confession of faith subverts the conception of the Church as the fellowship of believers. We recognise that those concerning whom Jesus said 'Of such is the Kingdom of Heaven' belong to God, and believe that no rite is needed to bring them into relation with Him. But many of our Churches hold services at which infants are presented, the duties, privileges and responsibilities of parents emphasized, and the prayers of the Church offered for children and parents.[33]

The following year M.E. Aubrey, the Secretary of the Baptist Union, produced through the Kingsgate Press, *A Minister's Manual*, which

---

[31] ibid., column 1.
[32] ibid., columns 1 and 2.
[33] E.A. Payne, *The Baptist Union: A Short History*, London 1959, Appdx IX pp.280-1.

contained orders of service for various occasions.[34] The order for the dedication of infants contains scripture readings from Deuteronomy 11: 18-20 and Mark 10: 13-16. These are followed by an explanation which spoke of the parents bringing the child to 'present him before God and His Church'; to witness their consecration to their part in the life of the child and to the high and sacred task of parenthood.

The claim of the child of a Christian home upon the prayers and services of the church is acknowledged. 'We welcome him as the Saviour, who is Lord of the Church, welcomed little children in the days of his flesh'. In so doing, 'we declare the claim of the Church of God upon the lives of those whom He has given to Christian parents'. Thus parents and church should labour together so that 'in the fullness of time and in years of understanding this child may be brought into the fellowship of those who serve and follow Christ'. Questions are then asked of the parents relating to their acceptance of their responsibilities as parents to nurture the child involving their own lives of example and the ordering of their home life so 'that this your child shall at all times be surrounded by holy living and Christlike example'. The minister takes the child in his arms, pronounces the child's name and then the Aaronic blessing, before returning the child to the father. The congregation is invited to join in the welcome of the church to the child, and to unite with the parents in prayer of thanksgiving by standing in their places. There then follows a prayer and the benediction. The dedication service usually is held, Aubrey suggested, immediately after the hymn following the Sunday morning sermon.[35]

This timing became widespread and remained so until the 1950s. It was far from ideal, particularly in the days of half-hour morning sermons, as personal memories of the late 1920s and early 1930s confirm. The result was delayed Sunday dinners and a rush to return in time for afternoon Sunday School.

Three years after Aubrey's *Manual*, the Carey Press at the Baptist Mission House produced *The Call to Worship*, by David Tait Patterson.[36] His order for the Dedication of Children was quite close to that of Aubrey

---

[34] *A Minister's Manual* compiled by M.E. Aubrey, London n.d. (but 1927). In the compiler's note Aubrey acknowledges help from members of the Baptist Union Publications Committee and from Principal Wheeler Robinson for his suggestions relating to the dedication of infants.

[35] ibid., p.18. Aubrey's Manual ran to a second, enlarged edition.

[36] *The Call to Worship*, compiled by David Tait Patterson, London 1930, 2nd edition 1931, revised edition 1938.

but made no mention of the timing of the service. It contained, however, no explanation of the service but suggested that the minister should do so in his own words. Patterson suggested also that the service might begin with the singing of a children's hymn. Memory suggests that this was usually 'God who hath made the daisies' – with its refrain: 'Suffer the little children/And let them come to me'. There was no suggestion of congregational involvement and response – but the final rubric stated, 'The child's name should be entered on the Cradle Roll of the Church'.[37] Reading the two services now leads to an impression that, whilst Aubrey's was a service assuming a close connection of the parents(s) with the church, Tait Patterson's was rather more open for what might be called potentially 'missionary' enterprise with parents more loosely connected with the church. Those were the great days of uniformed youth organizations attracting large numbers of children, many from non-church families.

By the end of the 1930s the practice of infant dedication appears relatively widespread amongst Baptist churches. As we have seen, its growth was due to parental pressure and the need for the Baptists to have some ceremony to balance the almost universal practice of infant baptism amongst all other churches. There seems not to have been very much theological consideration given to its meaning. The generalization of the 1926 response to Lambeth, mentioned earlier, was accepted without further questions about its ecclesiological implications being asked. That infant dedication had such implications was implicit in Rushbrooke's and Aubrey's involvement of the church membership and explicit in Spurr's idea of the ratification of infant dedication in baptism.

In 1932 a special committee was set up to discuss Union between Baptists, Congregationalists and Presbyterians. As we have noted, John Clifford's experience had indicated that a dedication service for infants might have had some positive contribution to make to Free Church relations. But the issue was not discussed at any depth and the general tone of the committee's Report to the March Council of the Baptist Union in 1937 is rightly described as 'negative'.[38]

But, so far as infant dedication was concerned, things were soon to change. Typically of Baptists, with pastoral practice well established, the necessity eventually became accepted of discovering what, if any, was its

---

[37] Ibid., p.149.
[38] By E.A. Payne in *The Baptist Union*, p.199.

theological and particularly its ecclesiological basis. Like Conrad Grebel 400 years previously, twentieth-century Baptists who rejected infant baptism now came to realize that they had to think through their theology of the child - which meant, of course, discussing their theology of what it is to be human.

If we look for a beginning of such thinking we can do worse than note George Beasley-Murray's article in the *Fraternal* of April 1943.[39] Starting from the question of a Lambeth woman to her Baptist friends, 'Why don't you baptize children, the same as other churches?' and the answer, 'Oh, there's not much difference, only we give 'em a dry christening', Beasley-Murray pointed out that Baptists should at least be aware of the theological issues which the practice of infant dedication raised and which on the whole thus far in the twentieth century had gone unanswered. In fact he might have added that thus far, they had been rarely raised. He pointed out that the importance of infant baptism in the Early Church was due to the prevalent notion of original sin which led to the assumption that a child was a fully constituted sinner, responsible for its sinful state and so liable to the penalty of eternal damnation. To this Augustine added, 'that the wills of all actively co-operated with that of Adam in his transgression, hence all were equally guilty'.[40]

Beasley-Murray suggested that, whether or not Baptists hold to the reality of original sin, few would maintain that the concept included guilt. Sin is not reckoned when there is no law, i.e. when it is not realized that deeds committed are wrong. After considering the question of whether an infant is naturally a 'child of God', he went on to suggest that children entered (became members of) the Kingdom of God in the same way that they entered His family - by faith. Thus the years prior to baptism as a believer were preparation for this event.[41]

The purpose of dedication therefore is to mark the beginning of such a process. Its meaning is threefold:

a)   A setting apart of *a child* by its parents for the 'nurture and admonition of the Lord'.

b)   A setting apart of *themselves* to the task of making it a disciple.

c)   A united seeking by the *assembled congregation* of the blessing of God on the infant.

---

[39] G.R. Beasley-Murray, 'The Church and the Child', *Fraternal*, April 1943, pp.9-13.
[40] ibid., pp.9-10.
[41] ibid., p.12.

Beasley-Murray concluded 'Our Service, then is a fitting introduction of a child to the community of believers in Christ. It is a practical remembrance of an unchanging invitation, "Suffer the little children to come unto me".'[42]

In April 1945 another distinguished Baptist scholar, Professor H.H. Rowley, wrote an article in the *Baptist Quarterly* entitled 'The Origin and Meaning of Baptism'.[43] Towards the end he turned his attention to the practice of infant dedication. He argued strongly in its favour and that it should have some clear and defined context which he was not afraid to call 'sacramental'.

His concern was that at the moment 'the services at which infants are brought to the House of God are still too sporadic and casual and are commonly given too shallow and too private a meaning. They are not regarded as a part of our denominational witness and practice, normal throughout the denomination'.[44]

Rowley agreed that, whilst the practice of Infant Baptism had little to commend it, 'we should recognize the truth it has striven to preserve. For there is room for a sacrament fraught with grace for the child, in its infancy.' This is, however, *not* New Testament baptism. Yet something more than a dedication service is called for. The child cannot make vows.

> But the parents can and should undertake in solemn vows to bring up their child in the nurture and fear of the Lord ..... If the vows are made and kept the child will indeed be blessed. We should cease to speak of it as an Infant Dedication service. It should be a service when the parents dedicate themselves to the sacred obligations of parenthood.[45]

But this was not all.

> It should be a service in which the Church is more than a witness of the parents' vows but a sharer in those vows and in the responsibilities for their fulfilment. It should be a sacrament of the Church and the Church in sharing in it should recognize the child as the child of its fellowship, in whom it henceforth will take an interest.[46]

---

[42] ibid., p.13.
[43] H.H. Rowley, 'The Origin and Meaning of Baptism', *Baptist Quarterly* XI, January – April 1945, pp.309-20.
[44] ibid., p.320.
[45] ibid., p.319.
[46] ibid.

On this basis the service was for Christian parents only. 'If this service is regarded as a Christian sacrament, it should be a sacrament for Christians'.[47] The church should keep a register of the children as the children of its fellowship and feel that it is involved in the fulfilment of the vows. Rowley argued that the statistics and care of children whose parents have solemnly undertaken the vows at such a service are of greater significance than total statistics of the vague category of Sunday School scholars.[48] It can be said that implicit in such a viewpoint is the concept of the 'catechumenate' which was to be advocated twenty years later and was to reappear fifty years on in the 1990s.

Rowley's final point related to anti-paedobaptism. It is not good enough to say that infant baptism is not what the New Testament says about baptism. The task of Baptists is to show another and better way of recognizing the worth of children to God and their relationship to the church.

> If Baptists can make this service normal throughout their fellowship and can fill it with richer meaning and ensure that it shall be taken seriously by parents and Church alike, they can make of their witness something more than the anti-paedobaptism with which they are too commonly associated.[49]

For Baptists this was to be a very big 'if' indeed. But Rowley's point is entirely valid and Baptist hesitations to heed it adequately can make them their own worst enemy in failing to proclaim a credible theology of the child and the church.

III

The first two decades after the Second World War saw Baptists striving one way and another to come to theological and liturgical terms with the infant dedication service.

Early in 1946 R.L. Child, the then Principal of Regent's Park College, produced a document which he entitled *The Blessing of Infants and the Dedication of Parents*.[50] In a very brief Foreword he spoke of 'the rapid spread of such service and the need for a brief statement calling attention to

---

[47] ibid., p.320.
[48] ibid.
[49] ibid.
[50] R.L. Child, *The Blessing of Infants and the Dedication of Parents*, London 1946 (pamphlet of 12 pages).

the theological and practical issues involved'. After a brief historical outline, Child went on to justify the service. If Baptists reject infant baptism as unscriptural, then we must be clear why our practice is based on biblical principles. He suggested the following reasons.

a) The service affirms the truth that all life is a gift of God and that the birth of a little child is a revelation of God's love and goodness to be received with thanksgiving and praise. Within this thanksgiving is included 'preservation of the mother in childbirth'.

b) The service expresses the value which our Lord set upon one individual human life from its earlier beginnings.

c) The service brings to a focus both the responsibilities and the resources of parenthood in Christ.

d) The service emphasizes the part played by the Christian community in the development of personal faith in Christ.[51]

These reasons are clearly in line with biblical thought and they are 'theological' very much in the pastoral sense. They do not, however, grapple with the issues which our seventeenth-century forebears faced and which are raised again by Beasley-Murray's 1943 article. For these 'reasons', Child argued for a pattern of worship along the lines of M.E. Aubrey's *Ministers Manual* and suggested a better title would be 'The Blessing of Infants and the Dedication of Parents'.

In dealing with the implications of the service, Child argued that it should be primarily for Christian parents but, at the same time, remembering that pastorally no request for the service should be turned down simply because parents are not church members. The request itself should be taken as an 'evangelical' opportunity. Even then, if the parents appear insufficiently responsive to the claims of Christian commitment, some sort of simple blessing and prayer can be offered within the home.

Child's final point was to become growingly significant. 'The service really requires us to revise our whole conception of the relation of the Church to the homes and families connected with it ..... It cannot be denied that in too many of our churches the Sunday School is still regarded as a separate organization ..... existing alongside the Church'. He called upon his readers to seize the opportunity of the 'popularity in our churches of the new

---

[51] ibid., pp.5-7.

service for infants' to put the Christian nurture of our children on a more satisfactory footing.[52]

What Child did *not* do in suggesting the title 'Blessing of Infants' was to indicate what he meant by the word 'blessing'. To some Baptists, probably too many, such language sounded like sacramentalism. Few had been able to agree with Rowley's statement of a year earlier that 'there is room for a sacrament fraught with grace for a child in its infancy'.

In March 1948 the Baptist Union Council approved a statement on 'The Baptist Doctrine of the Church'.[53] It was a succinct and comprehensive document which has not yet been superseded. Within the section on the sacraments, after sentences relating to believers' baptism, the statement continued:

> Thus we do not baptize infants. There is, however, a practice in our churches of presenting young children at a service of public worship where the responsibilities of the parents and the church are recognized and prayers are offered for the parents and child. Baptists believe that from birth all children are within the love and care of the heavenly Father and therefore within the operation of the saving grace of Christ; hence they have never been troubled by the distinction between baptized and unbaptized children.[54]

This was a statement relating to children upon which most Baptists could unite. But, of course, it begged a number of the theological and ecclesiological questions involved.

The origin of this statement was to meet a request from the Continuation Committee of Faith and Order, which was engaged in preliminary preparations for a World Conference on Faith and Order held eventually at Lund in Sweden in 1952. Amongst the subjects to be discussed were 'The Nature of the Church', 'Intercommunion' and 'Ways of Worship'. It was at this Conference that the participating churches moved beyond the methodology of comparing their views and listing their agreements and disagreements to an attempt to seek an ecclesiological unity by reflection upon the common biblical basis of the Faith belonging to all traditions.[55]

---

[52] ibid., p.11.
[53] Reprinted in Payne, op.cit., Appendix X, pp.285-91.
[54] ibid., p.288.
[55] *The Third World Conference on Faith and Order - Lund 1952*, report edited by Oliver S. Tomkins, London 1953, pp.15-16. See also my article on the 40th Anniversary of Lund, 'Swedish Milestone in road to Unity', *Baptist Times*, 13 August 1991.

The result was a growing consideration of baptism as a symbol of unity, of our being 'one in Christ' whose Body the Church is. An ongoing theological commission on *Christ and the Church* was set up which, as it developed over the years, found itself more and more involved with the question of baptism. Gradually as the sources were studied and early tradition examined, the Baptist position on believers' baptism came to be seen, not as an aberration of the minority, but as a practice universal in the first century and very common through into the fourth. When others took believers' baptism seriously, Baptists felt required to reconsider their attitude towards infant baptism and their own understanding of the relationship between the child and the church.[56] The Faith and Order Commission paper No 31 for 1960 contains the statement:

> We believe that the controversy between the advocates of adult and infant baptism is not a mere confessional controversy but must be seen in a context which makes apparent its true theological implications.[57]

No longer could the infant dedication question be taken on its own and answered solely in the pastoral context. Now it was necessary for it to be seen within the total ecclesiological context of entry into the church. The outcome was that from the mid-1950s until the end of 1966 the theological issues linked with the child and the church discussion came more to the fore in English Baptist thought and writing.

There was considerable literary activity on baptism in the immediate post-war years. Other churches were considering the question, not least the Church of England and the Church of Scotland, both of which groups produced significant reports. Within the British Council of Churches its own Faith and Order group were at work upon the question of Christian Initiation as a process. Baptist writers joined the discussion, amongst them R.E.O. White, G.W. Rusling, Stephen Winward, George Beasley-Murray, Neville Clark and Alec Gilmore, to name but a few.

Before we go on to consider what they had to say on our subject, two other contextual factors should be mentioned. First, the Liturgical Movement was a worldwide ecumenical enterprise but fostered and developed in England by

---

[56] See *Baptists in the Twentieth Century*, ed. K.W. Clements, London 1983, containing article by W.M.S. West, 'Baptists in Faith and Order: A study in baptismal convergence', pp.55-75.

[57] *Faith and Order Commission Paper 31*, Minutes of the Faith and Order Commission, St Andrews, pp.122-3.

the Joint Liturgical Group. Amongst other things, it challenged participating denominations, including Baptists, to re-think their patterns of worship and ask searching questions about the whys and wherefores of current worship practice. Naturally, baptism and eucharist could not escape some scrutiny and now, linked with the former for Baptists, was the service for infants, its form and place in the worship and its meaning.

The other factor was the widespread enthusiasm for 'Family Church' triggered off by writing such as R.J. Goldman, with his book *Readiness for Religion*,[58] in which he sought to define in children's development the 'personal religious stage', and N.A. Hamilton with his theoretical and practical publication, *Family Church in Principle and Practice*.[59] This latter book recognized the truth that during the late 1950s and early 1960s afternoon Sunday School was on the decline, due in part to changing Sunday 'habits' of the nation with growing mobility of families with their cars and the increase in Sunday 'secular' activities. It was this afternoon Sunday School decline which caused many Baptist churches to face the question seriously of the child and the church. Thus the seven years from 1959-1966 were the productive years of Baptist writings. We have space only to draw attention to some of these contributions.

In 1959 *Christian Baptism*[60] was published by the Lutterworth Press. This was a comprehensive symposium by ten Baptist ministers dealing with the development of Christian Baptism from biblical time to the present day. The concluding chapter was by Neville Clark on the Theology of Baptism. He argued for a clear distinction to be made between the children of a 'believing' family and the children of 'unbelievers'. 'The former belong to the sphere of the Body of Christ; the latter belong to the world which is marked with the seal of redemption and the humanity which, by incarnation, the Son has brought into union with Himself'.[61] Believers have responded to the Gospel, therefore their children will be specially related to the Body of Christ. But this relationship arises not so much from God's dealing with sinful humankind but rather from the fact of Christian marriage and the gracious Christian influences which will be the experience of the child in

---

[58] R.J. Goldman, *Readiness for Religion*, London 1965.
[59] H.A. Hamilton, *Family Church in Principle and Practice*, Wallington R E P 1963.
[60] *Christian Baptism*, edited A. Gilmore, London 1959. See also A. Gilmore, *Baptism and Christian Unity*, London 1966, esp. chapter 6 on 'Baptism and the Child' for a comment on the views of Clark and others.
[61] ibid., p.321.

that home. As baptism is not at issue for this child, there is no question here of *'insertion* into the Body of Christ', but there is a serious question of *relationship* to the Body of Christ grounded in the 'one flesh union' of two of its members. This should be marked by a 'solemn ritual' adapted from Christ's blessing of infants. The rite is not concerned with human vows but is concerned with the recognition and declaration of an act of God by which a child has been specially related to the redeemed community and with the claim and demand 'which that *opus dei* imposes upon church and parents alike'.[62] Baptists must face up to their persistent myopia in respect of the prevenience of grace.

R.E.O. White in the same volume dealt with baptism in the Synoptic Gospels and expressed the view that 'in none of these utterances [of Jesus] does the crucial question of the child's *relating* to the Kingdom of God explicitly arise ..... so far as his recorded words take us, the question is left open'. They are undoubtedly within the love of Christ but 'their entrance *into* the divine Kingdom and initiation into spiritual life is a wholly different matter, and far from indisputable'.[63] The following year White confirmed his view that 'so far as the child is concerned', responsibility comes with rational and moral apprehension; until it shall place itself outside that sheltered sphere, *'the child is safe within the love that saves'* [my italics. WMSW].[64]

In the same year, 1960, G.W. Rusling contributed a very significant article to the *Baptist Quarterly* with the title 'The Status of Children'.[65] In this he suggested that the Baptist argument against infant baptism was not over 'the fact that the paedo-baptist finds a place for the child in the life of the Church but that he wrongly transfers to the beginning of life the rite which belongs to the New Birth ..... and makes assertions ..... which distort and confuse the doctrine of the Church and Sacraments'.[66]

Rusling pleaded for the rediscovery and restoration of the catechumenate. A child of Christian parents will be under the influence of parents, home and church. He will be in the process of being 'instructed' in the Christian Faith. All this happens already to Baptist children. 'What we have not done is to make allowance for the idea of it in our theology of the Church'. The

---

[62] ibid., p.323.
[63] ibid., p.103.
[64] R.E.O. White, *The Biblical Doctrine of Initiation*, London 1960, p.122.
[65] G.W. Rusling, 'The Status of Children', *Baptist Quarterly* XVIII April 1960, pp.245-57.
[66] ibid., p.245.

church's ministry of evangelism and reconciliation in its response to our Lord's commission to make disciples required a catechumenate in its midst.[67] Although unbaptized, the catechumens are in a *creative relationship* with the Body of Christ, Rusling admitted that such a usage of the term and concept does not strictly follow the usage of the Early Church but suggested that the word 'catechumen' can properly be used for the children which we have in mind. He goes on to argue that the catechumenate should not be limited to children of believing parents - just as Sunday Schools are not limited. Both categories share the love of God and both have been born into a world for which Christ died.

1960 saw a pamphlet by J.O. Barrett on *Your Child and the Church*.[68] This was addressed to parents explaining that Baptists do not christen children nor do they ask for godparents. The responsibility for giving a child a Christian upbringing rests firmly on the shoulders of the parents themselves. Barrett suggested an order of service which was brief and to the point. After scripture sentences the minister indicates that all are gathered at the request of the parents to give thanks for the birth, to unite the prayers of congregation and parents for the guidance and strength of God in the responsibilities of parenthood and to ask God's blessing upon the child. There is then an acknowledgement of the claim of the child upon the prayerful interest and service of the church and a statement about the partnership of church and parents to the end that the child will 'freely choose the service of Christ and the fellowship of His people'.[69] The parents are asked two questions, the first relating to their gratitude to God in acceptance of responsibility for the child and the second inviting them to promise to surround the child by Christian example and influence. The minister takes the child and pronounces the Aaronic blessing before inviting the congregation to stand with the parents for a prayer. After the Benediction the parents should be given a certificate to mark the occasion.

There follow two sections of explanation. The first has to do with the meaning of the service, enlarging upon the content of the promises made and the part played by the church and parents together. For Christian parents this is an opportunity for the opening of a new chapter in Christian living, for

---

[67] ibid., p.247.
[68] J.O. Barrett, *Your Child and the Church*, London 1960.
[69] ibid., p.7.

parents who have not yet made any profession of faith it is a time to ask themselves about their response: parenthood is a God-given opportunity for them to enter upon the Christian life. The second part is pastoral in character and expands upon the meaning of the words 'A Christian Upbringing'.

Probably the most influential Baptist publication of 1960 was *Orders and Prayers for Church Worship: A Manual for Ministers*,[70] compiled by Ernest Payne and Stephen Winward. This manual became widely used and helped to draw to the attention of the Baptist Ministry some of the thinking of the liturgical movement. It will figure significantly in any consideration of Baptist worship in the twentieth century. The order for the dedication of children does not differ in general from that of Barrett, although it is slightly longer and includes most significantly the involvement of the congregation in affirming (by standing in their places) a positive response to a question - part of which reads:

> Do you as members of the Church acknowledge, and accept the responsibility, together with the parents, of teaching and training this child, that, being brought up in the discipline and instruction of the Lord, he may be led in due time to trust Christ as Saviour, and confessing him as Lord in baptism, be made a member of his Church?[71]

This sounds like support for the concept of catechumenate.

Whilst it may be said that Barrett's pamphlet and the Ministers' Manual both begged the theological question, their orders of service were an attempt to take seriously the growing number of requests being made pastorally of Baptist ministers to do 'something for the baby'. That was certainly the experience of the present writer, then in pastorate in St Albans, where such requests were frequent. In 1960 he had submitted an article to the *Fraternal* on the Child and the Church; this was published in January 1961.[72] Its emphasis lay upon taking seriously the church's part both in the Dedication

---

[70] *Orders and Prayers for Church Worship: A Manual for Ministers*, compiled by Ernest Payne and Stephen F. Winward, London 1960. Stephen Winward, who was a distinguished Baptist liturgist both in theory and in his practice at Highams Park Baptist Church, London, produced in the same year a brief order entitled the 'Dedication of Your Child', the pattern of which is largely followed in the manual.

[71] *Orders and Prayers*, p.126.

[72] W.M.S. West, 'The Child and the Church', *Fraternal*, January 1961, pp.15-19. See also *The Pattern of the Church*, ed. A. Gilmore, London 1963, pp.14-21.

Service and in subsequent concern for the child pastorally and in developing discipleship. The article argued that the dedication service was the point at which the church, which is the sphere in and through which the saving grace of Christ is made known in the world, becomes operative in the life of the child. Concern is expressed that the Sunday School in Baptist churches has often operated as though it ran parallel to the church rather than as part of it. Thus the dedication service is the occasion of relating the child to the church at the commencement of a *continuing* relationship which should be effectively monitored pastorally as the child moves on through adolescence towards baptism and church membership. To this end, it is suggested that the church's response to the question asked of it by the minister should be not only the standing of the congregation for prayer but also the verbal response from a church representative, whether Church Secretary, Sunday School Superintendent, Cradle Roll Secretary or whoever. It is important that that person should stand *alongside* the parents throughout the service.

The article continues with a reminder of the importance of bridging the gap between the dedication service and the age of commencing Sunday School or Family Church. There is a plea for one person in the church life (whether the Cradle Roll Secretary or not) to have responsibility for maintaining contact with the family and child. This is particularly so when the parents are not fully committed to the life of the church. The writer concluded by suggesting that the syllabus of the Sunday School needed re-examination and set out some suggestions for the content of such a syllabus. This is to be based upon the premise of the 'Sunday School as the Church in embryo' with the children developing their understanding of the Faith until the day when they are reborn into the fellowship of believers - the church. 'In this sense baptismal classes commence in the beginners' department and continue throughout the Sunday School'.[73] This teaching will seek to show the child its place in God's purpose in history and the church's obedient role in that purpose in guiding the child towards Christ and baptism.

What is again being described implicitly is the pastoral and evangelical imperative for the concept and practice of the catechumenate.

Dr George Beasley-Murray in 1966 explicitly supported the catechumenate idea. At the end of an article entitled 'Church and Child in the New Testament', he had a section on the 'Care of Children by the Church' in which he wrote: 'The secret appears to me to lie in the

---

[73] 'The Child and the Church', p.18.

catechumenate or, in modern terms, in an adequate system of Christian education'.[74] In a masterly summary, he had earlier shown how the catechumenate developed from New Testament teaching into a rigorous school of faith, with baptism as its climax. 'Its abolition after the Constantinian settlement when the masses swept into the Church and infant baptism became the accepted practice was of untold loss to the Church .....'[75] What is more, baptism should not mark the end of a child's Christian education but simply an interruption for an occasion for a response to God's grace which has been presupposed throughout the process.

On the theological question of the relation of children to God, Beasley-Murray commented:

> In my judgement we must have the candour to admit that the Bible gives us too little data to enable us to define with precision the relation of children to God, just as it has given us too little information to state with confidence how the parents of most of them - the pagans who have never heard the Gospel - stand in relation to God.[76]

Some may have argued (and may still argue) that the children are guilty for their condition as the children of Adam, while others have claimed that children are in redemptive solidarity with Christ, the Second Adam, until they fall out of it through their sin - yet it seems wiser to admit the limits of our knowledge. Because of this limitation and most particularly because God is gracious towards all children, the church should provide effective Christian nurture and instruction which is comprehensive in every sense, hence the catechumenate.

IV

At the suggestion of the Young People's Committee,[77] the Baptist Union Council in November 1963 appointed a small study group to prepare a statement on the Baptist view of the relation of the child to the church. It was urged that such a statement was greatly needed, first as a basis for

---

[74] G.R. Beasley-Murray, 'Church and Child in the New Testament', *Baptist Quarterly* XXI January 1966, pp.206-17: this quotation is from page 217.

[75] ibid., p.215.

[76] ibid., p.213.

[77] Minutes of the Young People's Department Committee meeting residentially at Dagnall Street Baptist Church, St Albans, 7-8 June 1963, reveal that the relevant suggestion was embodied in a resolution to the Baptist Union Council following discussion on a paper prepared by the Revd Bernard Green.

denominational policy, both national and local, in respect of children and young people, and also to contribute to the current ecumenical discussion of Christian initiation and the doctrine of the church.

Its terms of reference were fourfold. The group was instructed to consider the relation of children and the church in the light of:

a) The nature of the church as a redeemed community and a fellowship of believers.

b) The continuing mission of the church towards those who are outside and those who, although uncommitted to Christ, are already involved in the life of the church.

c) The different environments in which children of Christian and non-Christian parents are brought up.

d) The lack of recent study on theological and practical questions concerning children which Baptists are being asked in ecumenical discussion.

The report was presented to the meeting of the Baptist Union Council held on 8 March 1966, under the title 'The Child and the Church'.[78] Its contents were reported in the *Baptist Times* of 10 March[79] which went to print prior to the Council debate on 8 March. The Revd Geoffrey Rusling, Vice Principal of Spurgeon's College, was chairman of the group and the secretary was the Revd Harry Mowvley, who had had valuable and effective experience of Family Church at Cotham Grove Baptist Church in Bristol.

Whatever else may be said about the report, it tackled head on the issues raised by its terms of reference, not least the theological implications. No summary can do it full justice, for the issues are many and complex. We content ourselves, therefore, first by indicating its structure and then by drawing out certain salient points.

The structure of the report is:

    A. *Reasons for the Study*

        1. Denominational
            a) Church Practice

---

[78] Published subsequently as *The Child and the Church: A Baptist Discussion*, London 1966.
[79] *Baptist Times*, 10 March 1966.

        b) Church Doctrine
   2. Ecumenical

B. *The Child and God*

   1. God the Creator
   2. The Nature of Man and Work of Christ
   3. The Covenant
        i) The prevenience of divine grace
        ii) The solidarity of the family
   4. Christ and the Children

C. *The Child and the Church*

   1. The Catechumenate
   2. Children of believers and non-believers

D. *The Child as a Person*

E. *The Child and the Parents*

F. *Implications for Church Practice*

   1. Church and Home
   2. The Dedication Service
   3. Young People's Organizations and the Church
   4. Educational Approaches
   5. Evangelism and Children
   6. The Pastoral Responsibility of the Church
   7. Family Church and Sunday School
   8. Baptism and Church Membership

As can be seen implicitly and, up to a point, explicitly, the doctrines of the Church, Man, Salvation and the Sacraments came under scrutiny. In addition, a whole range of pastoral issues were raised. Whatever else the report illustrated, it made clear that discussion about the child and the church cannot be carried on without involving the whole gamut of Christian life and thought. Among the specific conclusions reached are:

1. Baptists have rejected the idea of infant baptism without facing squarely the problem created by the rejection of it.
2. To ask questions about the status of the infant or the child 'does not invalidate the theology underlying believer's baptism; rather we would say that theology obliges us to enquire further concerning the

questions with which it does not itself deal'.[80]

3. As a denomination we have hitherto tended to oversimplify our doctrine of the church as a fellowship of believers. While children are not *of* the fellowship of believers they are *in* fellowship *with* believers.

> We cannot rightly think of the living Church simply as a fellowship of believers. To risk an impersonal metaphor, that makes it as a garden considered apart from the nursery in which plants are being raised. In the history of the Church the classic name for that nursery is the catechumenate and the Church which is involved in the Lord's mission to the world always has her catechumenate and cannot be fully understood or comprehensively described without it.[81]

'The conversion theology which dominates Baptist doctrines of baptism and the Church is, in *itself*, silent about the infant'.[82]

4. The report goes on to discuss the biblical doctrine of Man and claims that simply to speak of the human race as fallen, in isolation from the work of Christ, is to violate the witness of the New Testament.[83]

The group, however, could not wholly resolve the tension which existed amongst the seven members between two views of the work of Christ. All believed that the work of Christ was for all, 'I Timothy 2:6': 'Christ gave Himself as a ransom for all', but the tension arose as to how that work of Christ was to be appropriated. All agreed that repentance and faith are essential for the salvation set forth in baptism but, whilst some group members regarded this as the response by which a person *becomes what he is* through his solidarity with Christ, others said that the response was a transition to *becoming what he may be*. This tension reflects that of the seventeenth-century Baptist which we have previously noted.

5. The report maintains that the children of believers and non-believers belong together in the catechumenate. It suggests that towards the

---

[80] *The Child and the Church* p.11.
[81] ibid., p.9.
[82] ibid., p.11.
[83] ibid., p.14. On this doctrinal point, and others, a group of Baptists, the Radlett Fellowship, published in 1967 a very critical response entitled *The Gospel, the Child and the Church*. See *Baptist Times*, 3 August 1967, review by W.W. Bottoms, 'Child and Church Report criticized'.

children of non-believers the church should act in the place of parents in giving the children a Christian upbringing. The dedication service is one of thanksgiving, the making of promises and offering of prayer for the blessing of God.

While clearly included are the children of believing parents, if other parents persist in their desire for a service in the church and in making their promises then they should be allowed to do so. In this case the *partnership* with the parents in the Christian education of the child is paramount and presents an opportunity of mission towards the home.[84]

6. An effective development of the catechumenate may result in more baptisms of children in the early teenage years. This is to be acknowledged and indeed welcomed. It is vital that all candidates of whatever age at baptism should be welcomed immediately into church meeting and given the opportunity of learning in practice the full responsibilities of church membership.

There is a remarkable silence in Baptist records as to the reception of and debate upon this Report in the Council on 8 March 1966. The *Baptist Times* makes no mention of it in subsequent reports of Council. The Minute of the Council carries no report of the debate at all and simply records the following resolution:

> That the Council thank the Committee for its report and believing that it deals with matters of great importance within and outside the denomination, whilst not necessarily committing itself at present to all the views expressed, requests the Secretary to negotiate with the Carey Kingsgate Press regarding its publication so that it can be subsequently circulated to the Churches for study.

Ernest Payne in his brief introduction to the printed report wrote 'The Council made clear that it was not at this stage necessarily committing itself to all the views expressed'.[85] He went on to mention the term *catechumenate* as 'unfamiliar to most Baptists' and, in the way the report presented it, as 'not exactly corresponding to the early Church or Reformation usage of the word'. He drew attention to the tension in the group on the issue of salvation reflecting the two streams of theology which have always been present in the

---

[84] *The Child and the Church*, p.34.
[85] ibid., p.4.

denomination. Some readers also might, Payne thought, at any rate at first, react against the idea that the customary Baptist definition of the church as a fellowship of believers requires supplementing. He added 'there are other matters which will not necessarily command agreement'.

Council members who were present at the debate thirty-one years ago appear united in the 'haziness' of recollection of the debate. All agree that it centred around the concept of the catechumenate which was vehemently criticized by some Council members. The Council also reflected the tension within the group on the issue of redemption.

What has largely been overlooked is that there were five recommendations attached to the Report. These were not included in the printed report and, so far as the present writer is aware, are not recorded anywhere apart from the minute book of the Baptist Union Council. The first one called for the appointment of a full-time qualified educationalist by the Union. The fourth asked for the publication of a pamphlet giving guidance on the dedication service. The other three deserve full quotation:

2. That any further statement of the Baptist doctrine of the Church should not only define the church 'theologically' as a 'fellowship of believers' but also take full account of the catechumenate including children found to be within the sphere of the church life and inseparable from it in practice.

3. That the Baptist Union through its representatives seek to initiate a study of the theology of childhood in the Faith and Order Commission of the World Council of Churches.

5. That the Council should take all possible steps to encourage churches to take full responsibility for all work among children so that separation between church and children's work be brought to an end and children taught and nurtured within the Christian community.

These recommendations were referred for further consideration to the General Purposes and Finance Committee. Remarkably there appears to have been no further action taken upon them. At least, there is no record at all of these resolutions in the minutes of the General Purposes Committee nor of the Young People's Department Committee. The rest appears to have been silence.

At the time a number of significant issues were occupying the attention of the Baptist Union. The 1964 Report of the Commission on the Associations was still being absorbed. The issue of Baptists and Unity was under discussion. The November Council of 1966 was to receive a full report on the 'State and Mission of the Denomination'. Conversations were proceeding between the Baptists and the Churches of Christ, and the Carey Kingsgate Press was facing financial difficulties. The denomination was also in the process of seeking a successor to Ernest Payne who was due to retire in 1968. On top of all this, Ernest Payne had a second coronary attack on 30 March and was out of action for several months.

It may be suggested that the group was given potentially too wide a remit. This resulted in them having to deal, in limited space, with a variety of difficult questions to some of which the Bible gives no definite answers. This was a recipe for division within a denomination as diverse as the Baptists. Certainly the report was too challenging and risky a document with which to face the Council. At that point in time the denominational boat could not wisely be rocked further.

But this is not to say that all was lost. Like many other reports to the Council some of the suggestions of *The Child and the Church* have been assimilated over subsequent years into denominational life. Children have been accepted more and more as, in a proper sense, belonging to the church, and this has included raising the question of their presence at Communion services. Baptist worship has reflected this. The infant dedication service has become integrated fully into the context of Sunday morning worship. It has also remained generally practised in the midst of a growing diversification of Baptist worship. Ecumenically now the practice of the blessing of infants in place of infant baptism has increased in a number of paedobaptist churches. There is a growing recognition on all sides that discussions on Christian Initiation in general and of baptism and church membership in particular must include consideration of the practice and ecclesiological implications of such a service.[86]

In 1980 the Baptist Union published *Praise God*,[87] which is a collection of resource material for Christian worship compiled by Alec Gilmore, Edward Smalley and Michael Walker. It contained a service entitled 'Infant Dedication and Thanksgiving' which seeks to recognize the variety of parents seeking such a service. The compilers stated their aim as seeking:

1. To combine a variety of diverse elements, assuming that the user

---

[86] See *Louisville: Consultation on Baptism*, Kentucky 1980, Faith and Order Paper 97, esp. pp.15, 18, 19, 105, 106, and *Baptism, Eucharist and Ministry*, Geneva 1982, Faith and Order Paper 111, esp. pp.2-3.

[87] *Praise God*, compiled by A. Gilmore, E. Smalley, M. Walker, London 1980, pp.129-36.

will select what expresses the emphasis he wishes to make.

2.   By pastoral initiatives to encourage freedom to act according to pastoral wisdom and Christian welcome.

Eleven years later another worship manual was published, entitled *Patterns and Prayers for Christian Worship*.[88] This was instigated by the General Purposes and Finance Committee of the Baptist Union of Great Britain because of the development of a growing variety of practice in Baptist worship. The chairman of the compiling group was Bernard Green. By now the title suggested for the service for infants was 'Infant Presentation'. Once again what was suggested reflected the wide use of such services and continuing variety of understanding on the part both of churches and parents involved. In fact, two alternative patterns of worship were suggested.[89] The first was entitled 'The Presentation of Infants' and contained thanksgiving, promises by parents and church, and blessing of the child. The second was called 'The Blessing of Infants' and was intended for those parents who wished to give thanks for the child but had no evident Christian commitment. The form of the promises related simply to teaching the child 'a good and true way of life'. There was a blessing of the infant but no participation by the congregation. This latter service was a pastoral response to a non-believing family's request for 'something to be done for the baby'.

Ecumenically, a Baptist liturgy for children has become growingly accepted as normal Baptist practice. Following on the 1982 Lima Convergence document, *Baptism, Eucharist and Ministry*, the Faith and Order Commission published *Baptism and Eucharist: Ecumenical Convergence in Celebration*.[90] Within this volume there are two Baptist contributions on Infant Dedication. The first is the already mentioned Order suggested in *Praise God*, the second is unattributed and is headed 'A Baptist Service of Thanksgiving on the Birth of a Child', which emphasized that it is an integral part of family worship with the whole church family present. It follows the pattern of thanksgiving and promises taken by parents and church but the questions to the church are specifically addressed to a lay representative of the church who responds on behalf of the gathered

---

[88] *Patterns and Prayers for Christian Worship*, Oxford 1991.
[89] ibid., pp.109-18.
[90] *Baptism and Eucharist: Ecumenical Convergence in Celebration*, ed. M. Thurian and G. Wainwright, Geneva 1983, Faith and Order paper 117.

congregation.[91]

In 1994 Churches Together in England encouraged the setting up of a Working Party on Baptism and Church Membership. The Working Party, which included Baptists, reported in 1997 on a range of issues. A number of recommendations were made, including one on the place of children in the church. 'We recommend that the renewed concern about the place of the child in the church with the Christian nurture of children and whole catechetical process should be tackled by churches working together'.[92]

Within the body of its report the group commented:

> Because of their understanding of the character of faith and church membership, Baptists do not consider it appropriate to baptize infants, but that does not mean that they regard the children of believers as being outside the household of God. Baptists believe that their ceremony of infant presentation and blessing signifies that such children belong to the Church .....[93]

The most recent basis for such a claim by the Working Group is to be found in a 1996 discussion document issued by the Doctrine and Worship Committee of the Baptist Union of Great Britain under the title *Believing and Being Baptized: Baptism, so-called rebaptism, and children in the church.*[94] The final four sections (X-XIII) deal with the question of children and the church. After a paragraph summarizing the present practice of 'infant presentation' which very much reflects that reached by Baptists in *Patterns and Prayers for Christian Worship*, the comment is made that 'many Baptists will regard the act called baptism administered to infants in other churches as actually having the same kind of meaning as infant presentation'.[95]

It is admitted that Baptist understanding of the relation of the child to

---

[91] ibid., pp.73-4. This service pattern was drawn up by Morris West; see above, p.11.

[92] *Baptism and Church Membership*, Churches Together in England (Publications), London 1997, para 39, p.17 (Dr West was involved in this, see above p.11). Earlier, in 1973, a working party on 'The Child and the Church' had been set up by the Consultative Group on Ministry Among Children of the British Council of Churches. Eventually the Working Party produced a 'consultative document', *The Child and the Church*, British Council of Churches, London (n.d.), which does not significantly deal with the fundamental theological issues involved.

[93] *Baptism and Church Membership*, p.17.

[94] *Believing and Being Baptized: Baptism, so called re-baptism and children in the church*, Baptist Union, Didcot 1996.

[95] ibid., p.39.

God and his church has often been vague and that it still needs a great deal of theological reflection and clarification. There are those Baptists who believe that children share the fallen and sinful condition of all human beings but that they are not reckoned as guilty until they reach an age when they can make truly moral decisions for themselves. Others affirm that being in Adam is not the only truth about human beings: they are also in Christ - the New Adam who has died and been resurrected - with resultant reconciliation with God. Children, therefore, are within the saving work of Christ until they reject or accept it for themselves by their responsible acts and choices. Many Baptists, possibly the majority, have not developed any theological theory about the salvation of young children but appeal to the mystery of the love, justice and mercy of God.

The document then goes on to pick up an idea suggested in the 1966 Report on the Child and the Church, namely that, prior to the moment of personal faith and acceptance of Christ and the responsibilities of membership of the covenant community, no one can be said to be a 'member' of the church, the Body of Christ. Nevertheless, 'children may be said to be "in" the Body in the sense that they are enfolded and embraced by it'. Such imagery is further developed by the group and the conclusion reached that

> we can develop the image of the Church as a Body in order to understand the inclusion of children who are not yet members ..... From the New Testament also we might think of the Church as the 'household of faith' *as a space in which people can dwell* in different ways. Because children are not yet '*members*', should not mean for Baptists that they are *excluded* from the Body or outside Christ.[96]

There is a further significant contribution to our subject as the group makes an attempt to give clearer definition to the meaning of the blessing of children in the service of infant presentation. The blessing, it is suggested, has a threefold significance. It is first a proclamation of the gospel, for the child shares in the blessing of being in a world in which Christ has risen and in which the grace of God already abounds. Secondly, the blessing is a prayer for the child that he or she will grow in the knowledge of Christ, and in due time come to a personal faith in him and be made a member of the church through believer's baptism. Thirdly, in uttering this blessing, the church accepts the child into the orbit of its influence. This is the orbit of

---

[96] ibid., pp.43-4.

God's gracious influence. This is true for all children, whether their parents are believers or not. Therefore the act of blessing should not be restricted to Christian families.[97]

As the twentieth century comes towards its close, it is encouraging that the influential authors of this report make this appeal:

> In particular, we make a plea for Baptists to think more seriously about the place of children in the church; we urge that the act of presentation and blessing of infants among Baptists be understood more clearly as a part of the journey of growing relationship with God.[98]

V

In an attempt to take seriously these concluding words of *Believing and Being Baptized* and also as a foundation upon which to build Baptist thought and practice into the next millennium, we would suggest the following conclusions from our study of the child and the church in the present century.

1. The controlling conviction is that the baptismal theory and practice of the Bible and early Christian centuries is that of believers' baptism. We are baptized on profession of faith into the Body of Christ, the Church. This has been the Baptist belief and tradition from its very beginning. It is now widely accepted ecumenically, as the convergence document, *Baptism, Eucharist and Ministry* attests.[99] It provides the context for Baptist theory and practice concerning the child and the church. Ecumenically, the more seriously Baptists take infant presentation, then the more effective they will be in proclaiming the truth of believers' baptism and the more seriously they will be taken by their ecumenical partners.

2. It follows that the responsibility of membership within the Church, the Body of Christ, belongs to the baptized believers. But it does *not* follow that, therefore, children are *excluded* from any significant relationship with the Church, the Body of Christ. As the 1966 Baptist Report notes, children can be *in* the Church without being *of* the Church. This viewpoint is echoed in the 1996 Baptist Report.[100] This is in no way an artificial distinction. As serious students of the Bible will know,

---

[97] ibid., pp.46-7.
[98] *Believing and Being Baptized*, p.48.
[99] *Baptism, Eucharist and Ministry*, para 11, p.4.
[100] *The Child and the Church*, p.9; *Believing and Being Baptized*, pp.41-5.

prepositions are crucial in determining the theological meaning.

3   The question of the status before God of such children has been, as we have seen, a divisive issue amongst Baptists from the seventeenth century to the twentieth. The reason for this, however, is that we are given no clear scriptural guidance to decide the matter. There have always been Baptist writers, from John Smyth to George Beasley-Murray, who have preferred an agnosticism on this issue. But all are agreed that such children are within the love and grace of God as reflected in the incarnation, life, death, resurrection and ascension of Jesus. If this be so, it is proper Christian obedience to act positively towards all children.

The distinction between the children of the believing and the non-believing parent has also produced much discussion. Here again, it may be suggested that scripture does pronounce definitely on such a distinction. Of God's purpose children are born members of the human race. The belief or non-belief of their parents does not affect their status of thus being born. The most recent thinking among Baptists counsels caution on discrimination against the child on the basis of the parents' belief or non-belief.[101]

4   Such openness presumes, indeed, 'optimistic' agnosticism, but it makes far more Christian sense viewed pastorally and evangelically. There is clear evidence that such practice in the long-term facilitates the working of God's gracious salvation to many a child and its parents. In any case, on what grounds has the church any right to bolt the door against a seemingly genuine doorstep request for admittance, help and guidance?

5   The method by which requests for infant presentation are granted will always be a matter of pastoral discretion. For the children of church families it is straightforward. For the children of other families it will involve discussion, explanation and assurance about the seriousness of the request. It can be useful for the minister to have a representative pastoral support group to share in this matter. This is not to erect a barrier but to make straight the way. How far the church will be reactive or pro-active to this pastoral opportunity will be a matter of individual decision.

---

[101] *Believing and Being Baptized*, p.47. See also the present writer's article, 'Infant Presentation: an affirmation of God's love', *Baptist Times*, 18 July 1991. Such a view in no way denies the *privilege* of being born into a Christian home.

What is essential is that the family is clear that the service of infant presentation is not simply a one-off day of name-giving and family celebration but a long-term commitment to relationship of home to church and church to home.

6. The pattern of the infant presentation service itself has been discussed already, involving as it does welcome, thanksgiving, responses by parents and church, and the act of blessing. On the basis of what we are suggesting, the question as to whether the alternative service of 'The Blessing of Infants' will ever be used remains open. It can be used as a 'halfway house'. But if infant presentation is to be taken as seriously liturgically, theologically and pastorally as we believe it should be, then the Blessing of Infant service would still require some form of subsequent presentation with responses as and when the relationship prospers.

7. The final point must relate to the follow-up to Infant Presentation. The church has accepted the child into the orbit of its influence. It belongs *in* the church. It is not enough only to present a certificate and write the child's name in a book or inscribe it on a roll. The church must accept its responsibility, it must have also people and structures to ensure that that responsibility is carried out.

The word 'catechumenate' may not be widely acceptable to Baptists for reasons which are not always clear. But the concept of it must be. Church growth comes about as much by the gradual incorporation of families into its life as by sudden conversions. But as plants need nurturing, so do families - be they one parent or two. The pastoral care and interest of the church is crucial. This is so whether the child is born into a Christian home or not. In all these ways the child will grow into the church, coming to believers' baptism and into the saving relationship of Jesus Christ as a member of His Church. The authoritative exhortation comes from Christ. It was he who said: 'Let the children come to me; do not try to stop them; for the Kingdom of God belongs to such as these.'

MORRIS WEST

W.M.S. WEST: BIBLIOGRAPHY

PUBLICATIONS

Fritz Blanke, 'Zollikon 1525: The Rise of the Earliest Anabaptist Fellowship', *Baptist Quarterly* 15.4 (October 1953), pp.147-65.

'John Hooper and the Origins of Puritanism', *Baptist Quarterly* 15.8 (October 1954), pp.346-68; 'John Hooper and the Origins of Puritanism *(Cont.)*', *Baptist Quarterly* 16.1 (January 1955), pp.22-46; 'John Hooper and the Origins of Puritanism *(Conc.)*', *Baptist Quarterly* 16.2 (April 1955), pp.67-88.

'History and Redemption', *The Fraternal* 94 (October 1954), pp.8-11.

John Hooper and the Origins of Puritanism (privately published: Zurich dissertation 1955).

W.M.S. West (ed.), *Evangelism and the Churches* (London: Carey Kingsgate Press 1958).

'Evangelism in the Early Church', in W.M.S. West (ed.), *Evangelism and the Churches* (London: Carey Kingsgate Press 1958), pp.9-26.

'Editorial', *Baptist Quarterly* 17.5 (January 1958), pp.193-6.

'Editorial', *Baptist Quarterly* 17.6 (April 1958), pp.241-5.

'Editorial', *Baptist Quarterly* 17.7 (July 1958), pp.289-92.

'The Baptist Historical Society', *The Fraternal* 109 (July 1958), pp.18-22.

'Editorial', *Baptist Quarterly* 17.8 (October 1958), pp.337-40.

'The Anabaptists and the Rise of the Baptist Movement', in A. Gilmore (ed.), *Christian Baptism: A Fresh Attempt to Understand the Rite in terms of Scripture, History and Tradition* (London: Lutterworth 1959), pp.223-72.

'Editorial', *Baptist Quarterly* 18.1 (January 1959), pp.1-3.

'Editorial', *Baptist Quarterly* 18.2 (April 1959), pp.49-53.

'Editorial', *Baptist Quarterly* 18.3 (July 1959), pp.97-100.

'Editorial', *Baptist Quarterly* 18.4 (October 1959), pp.145-7.

Baptist Principles (London: Baptist Union of Great Britain and Ireland 1960).

'Editorial', *Baptist Quarterly* 18.5 (January 1960), pp.193-5.

'An Oxford Experiment', *The Fraternal* 116 (April 1960), pp.16-8.

'Editorial', *Baptist Quarterly* 18.6 (April 1960), pp.241-4.

'Editorial', *Baptist Quarterly* 18.7 (July 1960), pp.289-92.

'Editorial', *Baptist Quarterly* 18.8 (October 1960), pp.337-9.

L.G. Champion, J.O. Barrett, and W.M.S. West, *The Doctrine of the ministry* (London: Baptist Union of Great Britain and Ireland 1961).

'Editorial', *Baptist Quarterly* 19.1 (January 1961), pp.1-3.

'The Child and the Church', *The Fraternal* 119 (January 1961), pp.15-9.

'Editorial', *Baptist Quarterly* 19.2 (April 1961), pp.49-51.

'Editorial', *Baptist Quarterly* 19.3 (July 1961), pp.97-100.

'Editorial', *Baptist Quarterly* 19.4 (October 1961), pp.145-6.

'Editorial', *Baptist Quarterly* 19.5 (January 1962), pp.193-94.

'Editorial', *Baptist Quarterly* 19.6 (April 1962), pp.241-2.

'Editorial', *Baptist Quarterly* 19.7 (July 1962), pp.289-91.

'Baptist Church Life Today', in A. Gilmore (ed.), *The Pattern of the Church* (London: Lutterworth 1963), pp.13-53.

'A New Look at the Christian Faith', *The Fraternal* 129 (July 1963), pp.10-12.

'The Evangelical Faith Today', in L.G. Champion (ed.), *The Communication of the Christian Faith: Presented to The Revd Dr A. Dakin Principal Emeritus of Bristol Baptist College on the occasion of his 80th birthday 21st November 1964* (privately published, Bristol: Bristol Baptist College 1964), pp.36-47.

Baptist Principles (London: Baptist Union of Great Britain and Ireland, revised edition 1967).

'Baptists and the Future', *Baptist Quarterly* 22.3 (July 1967), pp.176-85.

'Membership and Mobility', *The Fraternal* 149 (July 1968), pp.7-10.

'Random Thoughts on Preaching', *Preaching Today* 10.2 (Summer 1968), pp.3-6.

'Ministry Tomorrow', *The Fraternal* 161 (July 1971), pp.40-2.

Baptist Principles (London: Baptist Union of Great Britain and Ireland, third edition 1975).

'A First Report from Nairobi', *The Fraternal* 175 (February 1976), pp.17-22.

' "For what we have received ...": A Communication to Baptists' (President of the Baptist Union of Great Britain and Ireland address, London: Baptist Union of Great Britain and Ireland 1979).

'Towards a Consensus on Baptism? Louisville 1979', *Baptist Quarterly* 28.5 (January 1980), pp.225-32.

'Towards a Possible Agenda', *Review and Expositor* 77.1 (Winter 1980), pp.13-20.

'Dr Ernest Payne: Thanksgiving Address', *Baptist Quarterly* 28.7 (July 1980), pp.297-301.

'Foundation Documents of the Faith. VIII. Baptists and Statements of Faith', *Expository Times* 91 (May 1980), pp.228-33 (also published in C.S. Rodd (ed.), *Foundation Documents of the Faith* (Edinburgh: T. & T. Clark 1987), pp.83-97.

W.M.S. West and M.J. Quicke, *Church, Ministry and Baptism: Two Essays on Current Questions* (London: Baptist Union of Great Britain and Ireland 1981).

'Moderator's Notes', *Free Church Chronicle* 36.2 (Summer 1981), pp.1-3.

'Relationships - in the Church', *Free Church Chronicle* 36.2 (Summer 1981), pp.8-16.

'Moderator's Notes', *Free Church Chronicle* 36.3 (Autumn 1981), pp.1-2.

'Moderator's Notes', *Free Church Chronicle* 36.4 (Winter 1981), pp.1-2.

'An Unforgettable Occasion - and I was there', *Free Church Chronicle* 36.4

(Winter 1981), pp.24-5.

'Ecumenist of Our Times: Ernest Payne', *Mid-Stream* 21.1 (January 1982), pp.62-9.

'Moderator's Notes', *Free Church Chronicle* 37.1 (Spring 1982), pp.1-2.

To Be A Pilgrim: A Memoir of Ernest A. Payne (Guildford: Lutterworth Press 1983).

'Baptists in Faith and Order - A Study in Baptismal Convergence', in K.W. Clements (ed.), *Baptists in the Twentieth Century* (London: Baptist Historical Society 1983), pp.55-75.

'A Baptist Service of Thanksgiving on the Birth of a Child', in M.Thurian and G. Wainwright (eds.), *Baptism and Eucharist: Ecumenical Convergence in Celebration* (Faith and Order Paper 117; Geneva: World Council of Churches/Grand Rapids: Eerdmans 1983), pp.73-4.

'Baptism, Eucharist and Ministry: A Baptist Comment', *One in Christ* 20.1 (1984), pp.24-30.

'Methodists and Baptists in Eighteenth-Century Bristol', *Proceedings of the Wesley Historical Society* 44.6 (December 1984), pp.157-67.

'Tribute Given at the Memorial and Thanksgiving Service' [for Richard J. Hamper on 23 August 1986], *Free Church Chronicle* 41.3 (Autumn 1986), pp.8-10.

'The Bristol Tradition Then and Now: An Address given to the College Brotherhood' (Bristol: Bristol Baptist College 1986).

'40 years on' in *A Century of Promise: Hope Fulfilled (100 years of the Old Tauntonian Association)*, Oriel Press, Exeter, 1988, chapter 10, pp.96-104.

'Preaching Yesterday and Today', *Preaching Today* 32.2 (Summer 1989), pp.21-6.

'Preaching Yesterday and Today', *Preaching Today* 32.3 (Winter 1989), pp.8-12.

[written by but not credited to] W.M.S. West and M. Tanner, 'The Responses to the Baptism Section', in *Baptism, Eucharist and Ministry*

1982-1990. Report on the Process and Responses (Faith and Order Paper No.149, Geneva: World Council of Churches 1990), pp.39-55.

'The Young Mr Aubrey', *Baptist Quarterly* 33.8 (October 1990), pp.351-63; 'The Reverend Secretary Aubrey: Part I', *Baptist Quarterly* 34.5 (January 1992), pp.199-223; 'The Reverend Secretary Aubrey: Part II', *Baptist Quarterly* 34.6 (April 1992), pp.263-81; 'The Reverend Secretary Aubrey: Part III', *Baptist Quarterly* 34.7 (July 1992), pp.320-36.

'Lund Principle' and 'Toronto Statement', in N. Lossky *et al.* (eds.), *Dictionary of the Ecumenical Movement* (Geneva: World Council of Churches 1991), pp.633-4, 1008-10.

'The Legacy of William Tyndale', *Preaching Today* 37.1 (April 1994), pp.3-9.

'Churches Together in England: "Called to be One". Christian Initiation and Church Membership: A Report', in *One in Christ* 32.3 (1996), pp.263-81.

[drafted by W.M.S. West but not credited] 'Appendix B: Christian Initiation and Church Membership', in M. Reardon (ed.), *Called to be One* (London: Churches Together in England 1996), pp.67-70.

'Going, going - but not gone!', *The Fraternal* 264 (October 1998), pp.3-6.

'From the President: Ninety Years On', *Baptist Quarterly* 37.8 (October 1998), pp.365-6.

Baptists Together, Papers published in memory of W.M.S. West, JP, MA, Dtheol, Hon LLD, 1922-1999, prepared for publication by J.H.Y. Briggs and Faith Bowers, Baptist Historical Society 2000, which includes:

'The Child and the Church: A Baptist Perspective' in W.H. Brackney, P.S. Fiddes and J.H.Y. Briggs, *Pilgrim Pathways: Essays in Baptist History in Honour of B.R. White* (Macon, Georgia: Mercer University Press 1999), pp.75-110. Reproduced in the present volume with permission of Mercer University Press.

'The Revd Dr Morris West: Autobiographical Material', transcribed from audio-recording made by Dr West in the last weeks of his life. In *Baptists Together*, 2000.

'A few words about the Christian Ministry', from the address by Dr

West at the ordination of Anthony R. Cross, 18 March 1989 at New Road Baptist Church, Bromsgrove. In *Baptists Together*, 2000.

'Baptists Together: The Secretariat of the Baptist Union and effective denominational action - J.H. Shakespeare, M.E. Aubrey, E.A. Payne'. In *Baptists Together*, 2000.

UNPUBLISHED PAPERS

'The Lesser-Known Writings of John Bunyan', delivered to the Baptist Historical Society's Annual Meeting, Baptist Church House, April 1955.

'The Bristol 1526 Tyndale Testament: Its origin and its history', (n.d., unpublished manuscript in the Bristol Baptist College library).

'Churches Together in England: Called to be One. Christian Initiation and Church Membership. A Report' (unpublished 1995) [prepared for the 'Called to be One' process of the Churches Together in England, later revised and published in *One in Christ* 32.3 (1996), pp.263-81.

REVIEWS

Mr Pepys and Nonconformity, by A.G. Matthews, *Baptist Quarterly* 16.5 (January 1956), pp.236-7.

The Baptists in Norfolk, by C.B. Jewson, *Baptist Quarterly* 17.6 (April 1958), pp.285-6.

The Baptist Union: A Short History, by Ernest A. Payne, *Baptist Quarterly* 18.2 (April 1959), pp.94-6.

The Radical Reformation by G.H. Williams, *Baptist Quarterly* 20.3 (July 1963), pp.138-40.

The Northamptonshire Baptist Association by T.S.H. Elwyn, and *The Kent and Sussex Baptist Associations* by F. Buffard, *Baptist Quarterly* (January 1965), pp.43-4.

Christian England - Its Story to the Reformation by David L. Edwards, *Baptist Quarterly* 29.3 (July 1981), p.139.

Pastors and People: The Biography of a Baptist Church, Queen's Road,

Coventry by Clyde Binfield, *Baptist Quarterly* 31.5 (January 1986), pp.246-48.

Zwingli - The Positive Religious Values of his Eucharistic Writings, by H. Wayne Pipkin, *Baptist Quarterly* 32.2 (April 1987), p.97.

Melchior Hoffman: Social Unrest and Apocalyptic Visions in the Age of Reformation, by Klaus Depperman, *Expository Times* 99.11 (August 1988), pp.346-7.

FESTSCHRIFT

J.H.Y. Briggs (ed.), *Faith, Heritage and Witness: A Supplement to the Baptist Quarterly published in honour of Dr W.M.S. West* (*Baptist Quarterly Supplement* 1987).

Compiled by the Revd Dr Anthony R. Cross, Lecturer in Church History and Theology, University of Surrey Roehampton, London, February 2000. Dr Cross is grateful to Mrs Sue Osborne of the Ministry Department, Baptist Church House, for helping him to locate Dr West's contributions to *Preaching Today*, to Mrs Mary Barker, Librarian at Bristol Baptist College, and especially to Mrs West for allowing him to check some of the details included here.

INDEX

Aarhus, Denmark (F&O 1964) 10,22
Accra,Ghana (F&O 1974) 10,23,26,28
Accrington, Lancs 40,44,95
Adams, Theodore 70
Advisory Committee on Church Relations 84
Albert Hall 82
Amsterdam (WCC 1948) 10,63,71
Anabaptists 68,89
Anglicans 26,66,71,89
Angus, Joseph 41
Apostles' Creed 82
Arsenal Football Ground 3,82
Associations 18,36f,42,76f,80f,118
Aubrey, Peter (son of M.E.) 52
Aubrey, M.E. 1,4,7,48-63,64, 71ff,76,85,99ff,105
Augustine 102
Avon & Somerset Police Committee 11

Baldwin, Stanley 58
Bands of Hope 44
Bangalore, India (F&O 1978) 10,23,26f
Baptism 22-26,67,81,89,93f, 99,101,102,104,106ff,112f,115ff, 119,122f,125
Baptism and Church Membership (CTE Working Party) 121
Baptist Advance Campaign 60,63
Baptist Church House 3,7,9,13,40, 42,44,55,57,60f,69,73f,76,80,82, 85f,88,132

Baptist Forward Movement 4, 60ff,73
Baptist Historical Society 1
Baptist Insurance Co. 44,75
Baptist Men's Movement 80
Baptist Ministers Fraternal Union 97
Baptist Missionary Society (BMS) 6,17,46,60,61ff,65ff,71,74f, 77,80,82ff,87,100
Baptist Missionary Society Summer Schools 6,63
Baptist Revival Fellowship 78
Baptist Students Federation 63,69
Baptist Theological Students Union 69
Baptist Total Abstinence Union 44
Baptist Union of Scotland 80,83
Baptist Union of Wales 80, 83
Baptist Union 2,4,9f,12f,15,20,23, 35ff,39,40f,45,47ff,50,52,55, 57ff,60ff,67,69,71,74f,77f,83,85ff, 99,118
Baptist Women's Home Work Auxiliary 44
Baptist Women's League 44,50,75
Baptist Women's Shilling Fund 42
Baptist World Alliance (BWA) 45f, 50,63,67,69,77,82
Barker, Mary 132
Barrett, J.O. 58,69,70,79,110f
Barton preachers 94
Bateman, Charles 94
Bath 4
Baxter, Richard 62
Beasley-Murray, G.R. 22f,102f,

105,107, 112f,124
Bebbington, David 55
Bell, Ronald 82
Benskin, F.G. 72
Berry, Charles 53
Berry, Sydney 54
Biggleswade, Beds 65
Black, R. Wilson 55,57,61f,77
Blackwood, Christopher 92
Blanke, Fritz 8,20
Blomfield, W.E. 3
Boer War 43,45
Bonser, Henry 75
Booth, Samuel Harris 38
Bottoms, Ruth 29
Brackney, W.H. 1
Bradford, Yorks 17,53
Bradford: Westgate Particular Baptist Church 94
Bradford-on-Avon, Wilts: Zion Baptist Church 3
Briggs, J.H.Y. 1
Bristol *passim*
Bristol (F&O Commission) 10
Bristol Baptist College 3,5ff, 9,14ff,17ff,26f,63n,69,132
Bristol Bench 11f
Bristol Churches Housing Association 15
Bristol, University of 2,9,14,18
Bristol: Broadmead Baptist Church 92
Bristol: Cotham Grove Baptist Church 114
Bristol: Old King St Baptist Church 3
Bristol: Tyndale Baptist Church 2,14ff,18

British Broadcasting Corporation (BBC) 54
British Council of Churches (BCC) 11,21,55,107
British Faith and Order Conference (1964) 84
Britten, J.N. 61
Bromsgrove: New Road Baptist Church 30
Brown, Charles 35,41,51,57
Brown, Ernest 55,57
Brown, Mrs Charles 98
Brown, Mrs Ernest 75
Brunner, Emil 20
Bryan, Frank 58
Baptist Union Advisory Committee on Church Relations 10
Baptist Union Annuity Fund 42
Baptist Union Assembly 35f,38f, 42f,45f,48,52f,61,63,64,72,76f, 83f,99
Baptist Union Augmentation Fund 40,44
Baptist Union Church Extension 36f, 39f,42,44f
Baptist Union Commission on Associations 9
Baptist Union Commission on Baptist Polity (1936) 62,86
Baptist Union Council 9,21,36,38, 41,45ff,50f,58,60ff,64,69,72ff,78f, 84,86ff,101,106,113f,117ff
Baptist Union Discipleship Campaign (1932) 59
Baptist Union Doctrine and Worship Committee 121
Baptist Union Evangelism Committee 79

INDEX

Baptist Union Evangelist and Commissioner for Evangelism (Baptist Union 1935-8) 60f
Baptist Union General Purposes Committee 9,41,118,120
Baptist Union Home Mission Fund 13,36, 40,44,60
Baptist Union Grants Executive Committee 74
Baptist Union Home Work Fund 44,60,79
Baptist Union Joint HQ Working Group 13
Baptist Union Loan Fund 79
Baptist Union Metropolitan Area 63,76
Baptist Union minimum stipend 44
Baptist Union Ministerial Recognition Committee 75
Baptist Union Ministerial Settlement & Sustentation Scheme 44f,46
Baptist Union Pensions Committee 12
Baptist Union Publications Department 44,100n
Baptist Union Scholarships 3,7,79
Baptist Union Southern Area 76
Baptist Union Structure Group 9
Baptist Union Superintendents Board 12
Baptist Union Ter-Jubilee 1962 79f
Baptist Union Twentieth Century Fund 41ff, 47,49
Baptist Union Women's Department 58,80
Baptist Union Youth/Young People's work 9,44,53,63,66,78,113,118
Bugbrooke Baptist Church, Northants 66
Bullinger, J.H. (Zurich) 21
Bunyan, John 16, 33
Bush Hill Park, London - Raglan School 3

'Called to be One' Process (1995-) 11
Calvin, J. 21,91
Calvinism 90f
Cambridge 71
Cambridge: St Andrew's Street Baptist Church 49ff
Cardiff, University College of 12
Carey Hall, Birmingham 75
Carey Kingsgate Press 117, 119
Carey Press 100
Carey, William 41,68
Carlile, J.C. 41,46,50f,56f
catechumenate 104,109f, 113,115ff,118,125
Champion, L.G. 17,22
chaplains 86
Chapman, H.W. 8
Chapman, Herbert 3
Chapple, Lois 75
Chester, Bishop of 87
Child, Robert L. 6,8,58,75,104ff
Chivers, John 43
Chivers, William 43
Chown, Herbert 67
church membership 93,112, 115,119,125
Church of England/Established Church (see also Anglicans) 21, 54,87,107
Church of Scotland 54,107
Churches of Christ 61,119

Churches Together in England
  (CTE) 11, 27,121
Civil War 92
Clarens, Switzerland (F&O 1951)
  10,21
Clark, Arnold S. 61, 72,75,79
Clark, Neville 12,15,20,28,107f
Clements, K.W. 1,17
Clifford, John 36,42f,46,94,101
Coffey, D.R. 13,78
Collier, H.H. 66
Comber, Tom 68
Commission on the Associations
  118
'conciliar unity' 26
Conference on Politics, Economics
  and Citizenship (COPEC),
  Birmingham 1924 65
Congregationalists 37,49,65,
86,94f,101
Conservative Party 56,58
Cook, Henry 62f
Copenhagen, Denmark 70
Coronation Claims Committee 54
'Covenanting for Unity' 10
Coventry: Queen's Road Baptist
  Church 3
Cowper, William 74
Cradle Roll 101,112
Crêt-Bérard, Switzerland (*BEM*
  Consultation, 1977) 23
Cross, A.R. 1,30,95n,132
Cuff, William 43
Cule, W.E. 29

Dakin, Arthur 6ff,18,49,69
Davies, Arthur 82
Davies, Henton 9

Davies, Horton 8
Davies, Rupert 28f
Denominational Conference,
  Swanwick 1961 80,86
Denominational Conference,
  Swanwick 1996 80
Didcot, Oxon 13
Dodd, C.H. 49
Dodd, J.T. 66
Domestic Bench 12
Down Grade Controversy 59
Dr Williams's Scholarship 7
Dunning, T.G. 58

Early Church 102,110
ecclesiology 77,102,
  106,114,116f,119
ecumenism 10f,18,
  19-29,37,46,52,63,82,
  84,107,114f,123
Edinburgh House 66
Edmonton Baptist Church 3f,8
Edward VIII, King 54
Ellis, Alfred 55
Ellis, Robert 14
Enfield, Mddx 5
episcopacy 71
European Baptists 46,50,63,75
Evangelical Free Church Council 57
evangelicalism 26
Evangelicals 99
evangelism 60,62,63n,
  68,79f,110,115
Evans, Caleb 14
Evans, Percy 71,72,76f
Ewing, J.W. 43,49,77
Ewins, Thomas 92
Exeter Hall, London 46

INDEX

Fairbairn, Gordon 75
Faith and Order Commission, WCC
  10,19,21ff,53,63,65,71,106f,
  118,120
Family Church 108,112,114
Federal Council of Evangelical Free
  Churches 53ff
Festschrift (for Morris West, 1987)
  15
Fiddes, P.S. 1
Finch, Dorothy 75
Fisher, Geoffrey, Archbishop of
  Canterbury 71,82
Fletcher, Lionel 53
Focus Group (1930s) 58,69
Free Church Council 2,53ff
Free Church Federal Council 10
Free Church Union 53
Fullerton, W.Y. 49

Gange, E.G. 41
Garvie, A.E. 65
General Baptists 90, 93f
General Strike (1926) 48
Geneva, Switzerland 21
George I, King 2
George, Raymond 28
George V, King 54
George VI, King 54
German Democratic Republic 23
German Federal Republic 23
Gilmore, Alec 78,80,107,119
'Giving Account of Hope' Process
  (1971-8) 26
Glover, Richard 43f,46
Glover, T.R. 49ff,55,59
Goldman, R.J. 108
Goodman, Michael 48,49n

Gould, G.P. 95
Graham, Billy 78,82
Grantham, Thomas 90ff
Grebel, Conrad 89f,102
Green, Bernard 13,113n,120
Griffith, B. Grey 60,66ff,72,74
Hall, Neil 30
Hamilton, N.A. 108
Hardy, C.M. 66
Harris, T.M. 41
Hayden, Roger 1,10
Helwys, Thomas 68,90
Hertfordshire County Probation
  Committee 11f
Hicks, Douglas 9
Hiley, D.J. 43
Hindenburg, President 67
Hitler, Adolf 48,55,67
Hodgson, Leonard 71
Home Work Fund 73f
Hooper, John, Bishop of Gloucester
  8,21
Hubble, Gwyneth 75
Hubmaier, Balthasar 89
Hughes, S.W. 2f,57,77
Hume, Basil, Cardinal Archbishop of
  Westminster 10

India 23,68
Infant dedication/blessing/
  presentation 11, 89-125
Ingli James, J. 71
initiation process 24,99,107,114

Jackson, David 9
James, J. Ingli 58,71
Janes, Herbert 75
Janisch, Hubert 79

Jenkins, David 21
Jewson, Charles 58
Joint Liturgical Group 108
Juvenile Bench 12

Kettering, Northants 62
King, Martin Luther 78
King's College London 65
Kingdom of God 59,98,102
Kingsgate Press 95,99
Korean War 73

Labour Party 58,63
Lambeth 'Appeal to all Christian people' (1920) 52,54,65,77,99
Landels, William 36
Lang, Cosmo Gordon, Archbishop of Canterbury 54
Lay Training Programme, Bristol Baptist College 26
Le Quesne, C.T. 21,55,66,72,77
Leeds, Yorks 48
Leicester: Victoria Road Baptist Church 48
Lewis, W.O. 70
Liberal Party 55f,58
Life and Work (WCC) 53,63,65,67
Lima, Peru (F&O 1982) 10,19, 22,24f
Liturgical Movement 107
Llanvaches, Monmouthshire 92
Lloyd George, D. 55ff
Loccum, GFR (F&O 1977) 23,27f
Logan, Moffat 44
London Baptist Association 36
London, University of 36,65
London: Bloomsbury Chapel 36, 48,64

London: City Temple 42
London: Eagle Street Chapel 3
London: Highams Park Baptist Church 111n
London: Kingsgate Baptist Church 3
London: Praed Street Chapel 94f
London: Regent's Park Chapel 36
London: Salters Hall Baptist Church 82
London: The Downs Baptist Church, Clapton 65,72
London: Twynholm Baptist Church 61
London: Upper Holloway Baptist Church 76
Lord's Supper/communion/eucharist 93,109,119
Louisville, Kentucky (F&O Consultation,1979) 23f
Louvain, Belgium (F&O 1971) 10,22F,26
Lund, Sweden (1952) 10,21,106
Luton, Beds 75
Lutterworth Press 108

Maclaren, A.C. 42f,46,82
magistracy 11f
Malton, N.Yorks 35
Manchester, University of 9
Mansfield College, Oxford 8,49, 50,66
Marburg, University of 66f
Marnham, Herbert 43,46,48, 51,55,67
Marnham, John 43
Martin, Hugh 72
Methodists 2,28,54,86,95
Metropolitan Area 75

INDEX

Meyer, F.B. 46
Middlebrook, J.B. 58,71,84
Montreal (F&O 1963) 22
Moon, Norman 12,17
Morris, Sidney 75
Mowvley, Harry 6,14,16,114
Müntzer, Thomas 89
Mussolini, B. 55

Nairobi, Kenya (WCC 1975) 11, 23,26f
National Council of the Evangelical Free Churches 56
National Government 58
New College, London 65
New Testament 14,1,85, 91,99,103f,113, 116,122
New York, Union Theological College 49
Niceno-Constantinopolitan Creed 27
Nicholson, J.F.V. 19,23f
Northampton 2,3
Northampton: College St Baptist Church 3
Northampton: Mt Pleasant Baptist Church 3
Northern Baptist College 9
Norwich: St Mary's Baptist Church 36
Norwood, F.W. 53,57
Nottingham 39ff,4

Oecolampadius of Basel 89
Oldham, J.H. 66f
Olney, William 57
Orthodox Church 26
Osborne, Sue 132
Oxford 6ff,16,20,49,66,68,70ff

Oxford Conference on Church, Community and State 1937 67

Particular Baptists 91ff
Paton, William 66
Patterson, David Tait 100f
Payne, Alexander 65
Payne, Catherine (née Griffiths) 65
Payne, E.A. 1,6ff,10,17,20f, 28,48,58,62, 64-88,111,117ff
Payne, Philip 72
Penny, T.S. 46,48,55
Pentre: Zion Baptist Church 49
Pewtress, Mrs H.H. 75
Philip Griffiths 65
Pontypool, Mon. 17
Poole, Dorset 5
Presbyterians 101
Prestridge, J.N. 45f
Price, Seymour 55,66,72,75
Prince of Wales, Charles 10
Prison Sub-Committee 12
Probation Committee 12
Psalms and Hymns Trust 86
Puritanism 21

Rawdon Baptist College 3,49,69
Reardon, Martin 19n,28n
Reformation studies 8f,14,21,117
Regent's Park College, Oxford 6ff, 12,17,20f,29,36,48,64f,66,68f, 71f,86,104
Response to Lambeth Appeal (1926) 101
Rhode Island Colony, USA 68
Rickett, W.R. 39
Rippon, John 45
Robinson, Edward 43,46

Robinson, H. Wheeler 65f,68,100n
Roman Catholics 26
Rooke, Cecil 66
Rose, Doris 58
Rotary Clubs 12
Rowley, H.H. 103ff
Royal Air Force 20
Royal Commission on the Press (1947) 63
Runcie, Robert, Bishop of St Albans/ Archbishop of Canterbury 10,15,21
Rupp, Gordon 9
Rüschlikon, Switzerland 22
Rushbrooke, J.H. 6,50ff,67, 70,97f,101
Rusling, G.W. 107,109f,114
Russell, David 9f
Russell, Horace (Jamaica) 29
Russell Square (site for Joint HQ) 61,83
Russia 67

Schumm family 2
SCM Press 72
Separatists 89
Shakespeare, Alfred 42,55
Shakespeare, Geoffrey 39
Shakespeare, J.H. 1, 35-47,73f,76,78,86,88, 95
Shugnell, Leonard 73
Smalley, Edward 119
Smith, Gipsy 53
Smyth, John 89f,124
South Wales and Monmouthshire, University College of 49
South Wales Baptist College, Cardiff 12,49
South West Ecumenical Congress (Bristol 1976) 26
Southern Baptist Convention 70
Soviet Union 82
Sparkes, D.C. 13
Spiller, John 13
Spurgeon, C.H. 59,68
Spurgeon, J.A. 43
Spurgeon tradition 72
Spurgeon's College 71,114
Spurr, F.C. 98,101
St Albans 10ff,17,21,111
St Albans Council of Churches 10
St Albans: Dagnall St Baptist Church 9
'State of the Churches' (1944) 86
Stepney College 65
Sunday Schools 45,100,104f, 108,110,112,115
Superannuation Fund 73
Superintendents Board 75
Superintendents, General 30,45, 49,63,75f,80
Swanwick, Derbyshire 80
Sykes, Tom 53

Taizé, France (F&O 1979) 27
Tanner, Mary 10f,19,24,25n,27n,28
Taunton School 4f,20,49
Taylor, A.J.P. 57
Taylor, Adam 94
Taylor, Dorothy 9
Taylor, H.L. 6,55,61,77
Taylor, Ray 6,16ff
Temple, William, Archbishop of Canterbury 55
'Ten Propositions' 10
Ter-Jubilee Conference 80
'Towards a Common Expression of

the Apostolic Faith Today' (F&O programme) 27
theological issues 58,101f, 104ff,108,114,116f,122
Thomson, P.T. 77
Thomson, Ronald 85f,88
Tombes, John 91
Toronto: Yorkminster Baptist Church 9
Tottrell Bank 6
Turl, Stanley 11
Turner, Derek 9

Ulverston, Lancs (mistakenly given as Alveston) 6
United Council for Missionary Education 66
United Navy, Army and Air Force Board 86
United Reformed Church 26
United States of America 45,70

Victoria, Queen 43
Vincent, Samuel 38ff,41,46
Vischer, Lukas 19,22,28
voluntaryism 37

Wagner, Günther 22
Wales 92
Walker, Michael J. 90,91,119
Washington DC 70
Watford: Beechen Grove Baptist Church 84
Wesley, John 74
Wesleyans 37
West, Freda (née Metcalf, wife) 1,6ff,15,17,132
West, Griff (brother) 2,4.12

West, Joy (sister) 2,5
West, Meta S (mother) 2,4f
West, William E. (father) 2ff,8,12,16
White, B.R. 12
White, R.E.O. 107, 109
Wiles, Mrs O.D. 75
Wiles, O.D. 7,74,82,85f
Williams, Charles 40f,46,95f
Williams, Howard 87
Williams, Roger 68
Williamson, H.R. 64,68,70f,75
Wilson, Alec A. 82
Winter, Philip 6,16
Winward, Stephen 107,111
women 58,75,78,80,87
Wood, Henry 43,46,55
Wood, J.R. 41
World Council of Churches (WCC) 11,23f,26,28f,53,70f,88,118
World War I 47
World War II 4f,16,48,53,58, 63,73,76,104
worship 108,111,119,120

Yorkshire 17
Yorkshire Baptist Association 37

Zurich, Switzerland 8,17,20,21,89
Zwingli, Ulrich 21

Reports, Books and Journals cited

A Baptist Apologetic for Today (1925) 98
A Manual for Free Church Ministers (Gould & Shakespeare, 1905) 95
A Minister's Manual (Aubrey, 1927) 99f
A Pageant of Baptist History' (1939) 67
A Spiritual Check-Up (c.1959) 79

Baptism and Church Membership (CTE 1997) 27
Baptism and Eucharist: Ecumenical Convergence in Celebration 120
Baptism, Eucharist and Ministry (BEM) 10f,19,22ff,24ff,120,123
Baptist Handbook 35f,48
Baptist Magazine 38ff
Baptist Ministers Fellowship 13
Baptist Missionary Society Mission House, Furnival Street 40,60,62
Baptist Principles (West, 1960) 14,80
Baptist Quarterly 15,103,109
Baptist Times 114,117
Baptist Times and Freeman 42,50,53,55,97
Baptists and Unity Report (1967) 84,86,118
Baptists and Unity Reviewed (1969) 85
Believing and Being Baptized (BUGB 1996)

Call to Action (1935) 56
Call to Prayer (Free Churches 1940) 55
Christian Baptism (Gilmore, 1959) 80,108
Christian World 50
Christianismus Primitivus 90
Conversation about Hope (1978) 26

Fraternal 97,102,111
Fundamentals (by T.R. Glover) 59

Liberty in the Lord 78

Minister's Manual 105,111
Ministry Tomorrow 10

INDEX

One in Christ 11,25
Orders and Prayers for Church Worship (Payne & Winward, 1960) 111,121,123

Patterns and Prayers for Public Worship (BUGB 1991) 120f
Pilgrim's Progress 29,33
Pocket History of Baptists (c.1962) 80
Praise God (BU 1980) 11,119f

Speak that they go forward (BU 1946) 62

The Baptist Doctrine of the Church (1948) 77,106
The Baptist Union: A Short History (Payne, 1959) 79
The Blessing of Infants and the Dedication of Parents (Child, 1946) 104
The Call to Worship (Tait Patterson, 1930) 100
The Child and the Church (1966) 86,114, 119,122
The Christian Experience of the Holy Spirit, by H. Wheeler Robinson 65
The Churches at the Cross Roads 46
The Doctrine of the Ministry (1961) 86
The Fellowship of Believers (Payne, 1952) 77
The Meaning and Practice of Ordination among Baptists (1957) 86
The Pattern of the Church (ed. Gilmore, 1963) 78
The Principles and Practices of the Baptists (Williams, 1879) 95
The Report of the Commission on the Associations (1964) 86
The Times 87

What Unity Requires (1975) 26

Your Child and the Church (Barrett, 1960) 110